Growing Home

A Soul's Journey from Seed

Krystal –
I To an amazing woman
I have been blessed
to me again in this
lifetime. Thank you for
your friendship.
Love,
Leah

BY LEAH SEAN

Published by Sura Press
PMB 119, Suite 101
2950 Newmarket Street
Bellingham, Washington 98226

© 1999, 2001, 2004 Leah Sean

Cover illustration created by Jane Perini, Thunder Mountain Design,
    Sedona, Arizona
Cover concept: Leah Sean and Spirit
Author Photograph: Art of Photography by Jeanne McGee

Library of Congress: Copyright TXu 894-517 in 1999, TXu
1-021-387 in 2001, and TXu 1-134-681 in 2004

ISBN #0-9748864-0-8

Distributed by Sura Press

To order additional copies of this book, contact:

Sura Press   Sura Press
PMB 119, Suite 101   Monday–Friday 9am–5pm
2950 Newmarket Street   1-800-527-9104
Bellingham, Washington 98226

Acknowledgments

*A friend is one whom one may pour out all the contents
of one's heart, chaff and grain together, knowing that
the gentlest of hands will take and sift it, keep what is
worth keeping and, with the breath of kindness, blow the
rest away.* — ARABIAN PROVERB

A ceremonial embrace in recognition of friends and family
who were willing to take on the task of reading my manuscript
and to give thoughtful advice and guidance to my otherwise one-
sided view of the story.

I would like to acknowledge my son David who is a kindred
spirit. He took part of this journey with me in similar, spiritually
motivated motions, supporting my desire to finish this book by
his honest critique of content, flow and overall view.

I express my love and appreciation to Vincent who has been
a faithful friend through all of my travels since this story began,
encouraging me along the way. His message and comments on
my book add strength and the essence of true, spiritual family.

I thank the people that I drew into my life, family, friends,
acquaintances and lovers, for they have been my teachers and
mirrors who acted as catalysts in my growth to self-awareness.
Had I not loved them on a soul level, I might have moved out of
their presence and missed the grandest of gifts.

For those who have been my mentors, whose words of
wisdom have helped guide me, I am grateful. In the spirit and
purpose of this book, others' works have been quoted but not
credited, their names lost somewhere along the way. My
apologies and thanks. Know that your words became my friends,
my comfort and at times my counsel for the sadness and grief
that have been both my lessons and ultimately my gifts.

Dedication

To my unselfish and loyal cat friends, Kushi, Cali and Cassi, who quietly and bravely accepted the choices of my passages. Thank you for your patience and support and for giving up our play times.

Foreword

Countless books have been written as guides to successful living. Some have emphasized physical health, others have accentuated the spiritual. In addition, many have recommended the potential value of combining both.

The uniqueness of Leah Sean's contribution is found in her remarkable ability to encompass theoretical advice, amplifying and strengthening it by her personal experiential examples. Theory, plus practice and action, provide a synergy not necessarily found in separate areas. In her book, the dance between mind and heart, beautifully portrayed, suggests this union as the foundation of wisdom.

Leah Sean profoundly links the personal with the universal quest for enlightenment. In the 18 years of our friendship, she has continued to devote herself in the pursuit of awareness with the will to share and encourage all who have an open mind. In part, this was accomplished by the inclusion of some of the teachings of great masters of the past, combined with exciting presentations of living, significant individuals. Currently her experiences, often described poetically, illustrate how one person's life links to the timelessness of the human journey. As in the caves of our ancient ancestors, the images registered on rock walls speak to us and remind us of their existence. The embrace of mind and heart, past and present, the collective-individual quest presents the life force and its great mystery.

Leah Sean magnificently demonstrates that a great measure of life is not simply judged by the depth of one's fall, but by the arc of one's rising.

Finally, and most importantly, her journey shared through fire and light, extraordinarily reveals a great secret: that we, each and everyone of us, in truth are really great treasures seeking a map.

Vincent Mariani
Professor, Department of Art and Art History
University of Texas

The Earth is a mother of all that is natural, mother of all that is human. She is the mother of all, for contained in her are the seeds of all. The Earth of humankind contains all moistness all germinating power. It is in so many ways fruitful ... all creation comes from it.

— HILDEGARD VON BINGEN, A CHRISTIAN MYSTIC BORN IN 1098 IN GERMANY. HER COUNSEL WAS SOUGHT BY POPES, EMPERORS, KINGS, ARCHBISHOPS AND ABBESSES.

Introduction

*Do not follow where the path may lead ... go
instead where there is no path and leave a trail.*
RALPH WALDO EMERSON

This book is not so much about my life as it is about the
path that brought me to a state of self-realization and
awareness of purpose. It all began with a blank book, a gift
from my sister Connie, encouraging me to journal my
thoughts, experiences, dreams and quotes that had been
previously tossed into a box.

For years, I have been asked to write down my
experiences, and how I integrated them into a coherent unity
that guided me on the path that I walk today. There will be no
rules, no long lists of do's or don'ts, no brain drain. You are
perfect just the way you are.

This book is about each of us taking back our power,
tapping into our own knowing, then trusting that knowing.
Chosen life experiences guide us to remember and seek
always for the answers within. Do not allow others to
influence us by their choices. Think for yourself. Don't
believe anything I say. Use your own filtering system to
discern what is right for you. Discovering who you are not
guides you to who you are.

What if we take the literal meaning out of the words and
go by the intent in our hearts? Your experience with a word
and an emotion may be different than mine, so when it is
used, we are immediately at odds. When we can get past the
words and listen only to the intent, there will be open

communication. If these words stir something within you to agreement, anger or disbelief, then they have fulfilled their purpose.

The premise of this book is that all of the answers we seek are already within us, waiting to be remembered. When I perceive a possibility for me and my perception shifts, the answer shifts. Much like the parables in the Bible, we see at the level of awareness that we have achieved at that time. In taking this journey with me, I hope my experiences will act as a catalyst to encourage you on your quest to self. All I can promise you is that it will be an amazing journey.

ℙ

Growing Up

The seed, custodian of all possibilities, is full and precious

Through my growing up and marriage, my Divine Seed was ripening, developing, completing my soul's agreed-upon script. When it became full and precious, I left my marriage to disperse the seeds of wisdom while living the life of my soul's expression.

The seeds of possibility came to express through a human body here on Earth, laying dormant as the soul's journey through this physical world took place, preparing the seed to burst forth with the gifts of the soul. In the beginning, there is childhood, a state of being, absorbing everything.

My alpha point of this incarnation began in 1934, the daughter of parents from small farming communities in western Nebraska. Although the social consciousness was a little rigid at that time, I came away with a good set of values

that have served me well in this life. And so my life began
with hard-working, earthy parents and an older sister Connie.

My dad, his two brothers and youngest sister made up the
group called the Royal Hawaiians, consisting of an electric
guitar, guitar, banjo and bass. They traveled and performed
mostly in the state of Nebraska, until their families grew,
requiring a more stable way of life. There were no jobs
available in the small community of York, so the decision was
made to move to Omaha where my sister and I were raised.
The families arrived in the big city of Omaha with faith,
trust, and barely enough money to feed everyone, let alone
pay the rent.

A short time after moving to Omaha, my dad made the
fortunate decision to work for a Ford dealer who later sold
the business to my dad and his two brothers, giving them a
lucrative income until they retired at very young ages.

I have such happy memories of being held on Dad's lap
as he sang and played his guitar, as he encouraged us to
honor our bedtime. This took a bit of coaxing since Lux
Video Theater, one of our favorite radio shows was just
starting at bedtime. Although I never asked, it is now obvious
that they were aware of our presence as we crawled closer to
the living room to listen to the show. Our lives were very
simple and uncomplicated at that time.

A wonderful, creative cook, Mom always had full,
delicious meals that were made from scratch. She was well-
read, active in the community and also a gifted seamstress,
a necessary quality since we lived on smaller means in
those days.

Dad raised the most beautiful tea roses. Often he would
cut a vividly colored one to bring to Mom, patting her on the

bottom as he gave her a kiss. This is one of the very tender and endearing memories I have and hold on to.

A steamer trunk once used to move my mother's clothing for college, stored in the attic, became a treasure trove of old clothes and pictures. I still remember the smell of the moth balls that protected and permeated an old, woolen uniform of Dad's and a sexy 1930s dress that Mom had saved. Connie and I could be anyone anywhere in the magic of the moment. Many hours were spent in what became expanded consciousness, what I call imaginative play, in that musty attic in the old house on Larimore Street.

Cutting pictures of food out of magazines, Connie would set up a restaurant with menus and serve anyone who was willing to participate in our play. Usually, it was Dad who had just arrived home very tired and hungry. He encouraged our love for food which later brought Connie to become a dietitian and me to major in foods. Sometimes we took our desire for food a step further, combining dirt and water to make mud pies, baking them in the sun, then eating them like cakes. It seems that we intuitively found a way to ingest minerals that may have been lacking in our diets.

Our holidays were filled with love, confusion and gourmet food prepared by my mom and two aunts. Most of the time, there were six adults and 10 children, but on occasion, there would be as many as 30 family members from grandparents to babies.

The men and boys retired to the couch or the floor to watch football while the women and girls cleaned up, doing dishes by hand, rotating the dish towels as they became soaked. None of us owned a dishwasher in those days. I must admit to complaining a bit, but the truth was that we were all together in the supportive atmosphere of a big family with time to express our feelings and receive loving guidance. I was very blessed. The times spent with my sister and cousins appeared to be innocent, non-directed play, but the reality is that we were each experiencing self and limits of self within the confines of safety and love of family.

With a Ping-Pong table and a source of music in our basement, our home became the gathering place for classmates and friends. Another and maybe more important reason may have been the generous offerings of stacks of cold meat, cheeses, loaves of bread and plenty of sodas that were always available to satisfy the ongoing hunger of teenagers. Although there was no awareness at that time, we were blessed with more financial abundance than most of our classmates.

My friends loved and admired my father for his wisdom and willingness to share his time, especially the boys who were eager for male guidance. My dad was tall, handsome and had a great sense of humor. Everyone liked him. When he died at the young age of 58, a true and kindred spirit was taken from my life. He had touched so many lives with his kind and generous way of living that his memory is one of fulfilled promises and purpose.

I felt complete with Dad before he left the Earth. But Mom and I had our differences, maybe because I had the most to learn from her. Two years after Mom died, she appeared in an awake dream where we hugged, cried and acknowledged our love for each other.

Wanting to speak my truth to someone about my other-worldly experiences, I was left with the only alternative of going inside myself. Often I spent hours swinging on our backyard rope or rocking on the bed until reaching a state of meditation. To me, meditation is a state of mind where there is no other, we are all one. Defining this state of mind is "like trying to explain inspiration," as my friend Vincent would say.

Longing to reconcile who I am in the family, my feeling was that I must have been adopted, a question I often asked my mother. At four I asked my mom where the sun and moon came from and how the stars remained up in the sky. I think she felt overwhelmed and confused having such a daughter.

A poem I wrote as a junior in high school has, for the first time, become an experience-filled understanding of the true meaning of the words that flowed from me. Even at the age of 16 my thoughts were reflective.

Life's Tasks

The straight, sheltered path of an arrow is easy to follow,
protected by loving hands.
Shot on the long, sinuous path, the world collapses,
the heart broken gives in.
Understanding life not as a vagrant living off the Earth,
but employed in the art of life's tasks ...
mature and understanding.

Entering college with courage and some experience gained from life up to this point, a very perplexing four years were ahead of me. There were bursts of enthusiasm amidst great confusion. Being a bit of a rebel, like a Marlboro woman taking my own path, still on wobbly, unsure legs, I did my best to complete the agreement with my dad to attend college for at least two years. I completed four.

Graduating from college with a Bachelor of Science degree in foods, I decided to get married the following December instead of finishing my education as a dietitian. My parents soon found that I could not be dissuaded from my intent to marry, supporting my unwavering decision by planning and paying for a beautiful wedding. After the wedding, we moved immediately to the East Coast where my husband was stationed at Andrews Air Force Base.

Obvious from the very beginning was my husband's high level of self-interest. My pattern of the disease-to-please was to bring a big awakening very early in my marriage. My friend William David said that it is all a little joke, not marriage but the reasons most of us get together. We feel like we just can't live without this person and wake up later wondering why we chose this relationship. Twice I left and went home, only to return to my marriage, still feeling drawn to my husband's energy. I woke up more than once, looking over at him in bed, and felt shocked to be married to a stranger. My unspoken thoughts to him were: "I honor your free will as I honor my own. I will move forward even though I may walk alone."

May I say that these times of more challenging choices are always in good order, but at the time, I wasn't aware of this wisdom. I felt like an acquisition, being offered a cold, detached demeanor. I allowed my husband to dishonor me. That wasn't part of the agreement.

No matter how uncomfortable the situations, I tried my best to work through them, finding that the harder I tried, the more he resisted. Only when I was brutally honest, recognizing the part that I played in this dysfunctional relationship, was I able to stand outside myself as an observer to see the truth. Once I got the message that there are no victims, I owned my choices as self-directed toward healing and took my power back.

As memories of other tumultuous lifetimes with him came into my conscious mind, some with the help of psychic friends and some from my own inner knowing, I began to get the bigger picture. We came together again to complete or balance energies from the past, which is also the present. I was told that marriage was not a destination, but a process. Once the purpose of the attraction that drew me to my husband was fulfilled, I turned my life around, followed the guidance of my soul and left my 27 year marriage.

I had always loved children so I was overjoyed when my son David came into my life. Five years later my daughter Ann joined us for this great adventure in family life. I was blessed with the presence of these two souls who came to remind me of who I am. I made it possible for them to contact this world for the sake of their evolution, allowing me to be their temporary guide during the early stages of their lives.

Although I was living with my yet unrecognized dysfunctions, I loved my children and gave them spiritual, mental and physical guidance to the best of my ability. My higher self knew that, as a mother, I was taking on the role to assist them through their young lives, always guided by the voice of their own higher selves. They were making their own choices and fulfilling the gifts of their souls by creating a better place in the world. This all sounds perfect but there were and still are misunderstandings and miscommunications in our relating with each other. All I know is that I love and support them in the process of fulfilling themselves and their purposes here on Earth.

As a stay-at-home mother I volunteered which gave me the opportunity to serve the community and to fulfill my interests in other areas. Being a homeroom mother chaperoning outside school activities allowed me to meet David and Ann's classmates and to let them know that I was interested in not only loving them but also in their lives and experiences. Most importantly, I was always home when they got out of school.

I worked with my husband who was a lawyer typing wills, adoptions and estates. I also dabbled in interior design, almost completely redoing our last residence in a Greek-like setting and losing myself in gourmet cooking and entertaining, much to my delight.

Despite my husband's lack of interest in redoing and decorating our newly moved into older house, I started knocking out walls leaving, of course, the support beams. Voil'a, the beginning! Obviously, I needed professional help to take out dry wall, move electrical outlets and carve the curved railing up to the second floor. My creative juices started flowing and, by the time it was complete, there was a hand-carved, curved railing supported by Lucite spindles to look like it was floating; archways into the living room and a new arched opening into the den, and Roman columns into the living room, and new German kitchen cupboards.
I eliminated the fifth bedroom above the entry, which created a two-story high space with a large sky light and plant decks encircling the entry. I had never felt so alive!

Just as I was asked to be president of the Omaha Women's Town Hall that I had participated in for five years, my husband was transferred to Chicago. My interests took second place to my husband's choices in his job. I was always starting over.

After moving to Lake Barrington Shores near Chicago I started another town hall, choosing speakers who were other-worldly and spiritual to be my guest speakers, including Dr. J. Allen Hynek, noted scientist and professor of astronomy at the University of Illinois and former head of

Project Blue Book, who was a consultant on the movie Close
Encounters of the Third Kind. Another noted speaker was M.
B. Dykshoorn, a clairvoyant in all five senses and accepted by
police departments all over the world as a crime scene
investigator. Sir Edmund Hillary, a courageous man on all
levels, the first to climb Mount Everest, stood before me as a
mutual friend introduced us. Not a word was spoken. Just by
his presence, a gift of great magnitude was bestowed upon
me. His powerful, grounded energy reflected back to me the
obvious truth of the protective façade that I had been
expressing through. I was shocked, humbled and grateful for
this meeting which acted as a catalyst, bringing me back full
circle to the unpretentious time in my life just before entering
high school. Some bestow their gifts upon us by their
presence, in total silence.

In Chicago I found a large hospital that needed a
volunteer for a position in the surgical hold area where
patients were brought to wait for a surgical procedure.
I checked them in and made sure that the patient, procedure
and doctor were coordinated. Two days a week I drove
downtown, arriving at the hospital at 7 a.m., donned nurses
greens and surgical covers for my shoes and sat at my
appointed station outside of the operating rooms. The first
day I became aware that this job called for more than being
an observer and coordinator. Patients who had just been
separated from loved ones and brought to a cold, unfamiliar
place for an unknown procedure were understandably scared.
Holding hands and listening to their fears quickly became
part of my job.

My intent was to serve, but it soon became obvious that I
was also being served. In the vulnerability and loss of control
of self, especially in the anticipation of an operation, their

emotions often turned to anger which was expressed to the safest person, me. After a few months, being an empath, I was drained from the emotions and situations that I had no control over, so I quit.

This experience helped me to reevaluate my choices at this point in life. My soul was urging me to fulfill my purpose and complete the agreement made before coming into this embodiment. Time for a change.

Leaving my marriage represented stepping outside of family dynamics, removing myself from the games we played. At first it was like pulling the cork from a champagne bottle, a powerful pulling away from, then a pop and the cork and I were free. As I separated from my family and the role that I played, anger and blame were focused on me, the disrupter.

After my childhood, 27 years of marriage and raising two children, I had grown beyond societal and family expectations of who I should be and the denial of who I am. Having played the role of daughter, sister, wife and mother, I was now free to be me.

It was time to break out of old modes of behavior and move on. David was out of college, living and working in Mississippi. Ann was in her senior year of college and very willing to be on her own, or so she said. I filed for divorce and headed for Austin, Texas settling in with a blanket, a pillow and a few personal items.

Knowing that leaving my marriage was only one step in finding myself, the real adventure of discovery began. In November 1983, my further search for self and purpose extended into a long, questing journey filled with valuable lessons, needed skills for life and the blessings of the profound souls that I encountered along the way.

It is called growing up. As children, most of us had a very idealistic view of people and what the world of illusion had to offer, especially in my era. Interestingly enough, after living life for 69 years, I have come full circle back to looking at life as though through the eyes of a child, only now with the experience and knowing of an adult.

Even though I express as a loner, I have always loved people, feeling deep concern for their well being. With no understanding at the time, I felt compassion for those who stood outside school and social activities. I lived in both worlds, popular and unpopular, learning the most from the courage of those who were expressing themselves from their lack of self-love. I have no desire to go back to that time, but the memories are good and loving, the lessons relevant and necessary for me to grow and ultimately remember who I am.

The life that was being offered to me felt so foreign that I started keeping my thoughts to myself, staying in communion with nature and animals where it was possible to connect with the inner purity of my soul.

This is not to say that my childhood was unhappy. Every family has its dysfunctions, mine being no different. These feelings had more to do with my own personal, inner self not being able to express fully in this consciousness.

During one of the counseling sessions I went to after leaving my marriage, I was told that any quality in my husband that pushed a button in me, was acting as a mirror for my acknowledgement. This didn't sit well at first, but after taking a long, hard and honest look, I came to know that the advice was right on. Soon, but not overnight, I felt the purity of soul love for him, though there was no desire to have him in my life anymore. I was finally at peace with myself and able to move on with my own life.

Personal will working with ego may lead to stubbornness and arrogance.
Will working with spirit guides our way back to true self offering the gifts of our souls, to lift humanity past, present and future, forever.

Texas

The fertile earth is prepared to receive the seed

A willingness to live in the sometimes uneasiness of a void, welcomes and allows the new to then fill the emptiness with the results of the growth that has taken place.

Sometimes the most daring step to freedom is walking out the front door. My step out the front door took place as I moved to Austin, Texas, a city unfamiliar to me. I was embarking on a journey of self-gratitude and self-awareness that would be both inspiring and, at times, painful.

Saying good-bye to my family in Nebraska was so emotional that I was in a physical and mental daze, feeling outside myself like a robot going through the motions. I was not emotionally available to connect with my family's feelings about my departure. It seems the unspoken message to keep a stiff upper lip was prevalent in my childhood, in my marriage and even now in my leaving.

I was so ready to be on my own that I drove without stopping, except for food, from Lincoln, Nebraska to Austin, Texas. The journey to outward freedom was joyful and went smoothly. The journey to inward freedom was just beginning.

Arriving in Austin, moving into my new apartment with my own thoughts, free from other ideas and opinions, a great dichotomy was revealed ... the sweet taste of freedom and a heavy load of anger and dysfunctional emotions to be dealt with, processed, and released. It was a time of great confusion, both outer and inner. On the journey toward finding and loving myself, there was a lack of self-love to work through. I was actually beginning to get a glimpse of great joy and I loved it. Coming from the belief that everything is the Divine reaching out to love and heal us, the decision was made to try my wings by being who I am, to the extent that I could at that time. Placing myself in many unfamiliar places and circumstances for the first time in life, I was making choices according to my own desires, not within the confines of my parents rules and lifestyle or from the needs of my husband and my children. I chose many paths in order to find my way by the process of elimination.

> *Scripture leaves it to us to discover the secret that when we are courageous enough to risk being free and creative, breaking out of old modes of behavior, we will experience great joy. Those who avoid change, who fear the pain of rebelling and beginning again so much as to not begin at all, are not ready for the life which Jesus calls the Kingdom of God.* — ASHA STAGER

Speaking my own truth to find the boundaries of self,
I was sometimes asked to leave a group that I perceived felt
threatened by me. I had lost nothing and gained everything.
I went into these groups open to learn, but not willing to join
in being a follower or to participate in something that carried
energies harmful to others and our higher consciousness. It
was becoming obvious, as I gained love for self, that all
situations and people who were not loving and supportive of
the choices that I made for myself had no place in my life
anymore. This didn't happen overnight.

I remember in college my English professor gave us an
assignment to read and find our own meaning in a certain
poem. Delighted to be called on the next day, I shared my
thoughts on my interpretation. With no further explanation,
the professor immediately called on another student. I felt
deflated and shocked knowing that, from his abrupt
demeanor, he was dismissing me.

A similar experience took place in my chemistry class.
Preparing for a test, I asked the teacher for an explanation of
how a formula worked. Unfortunately, she didn't know or
understand the process either, though she was asking me to
memorize the formula. I felt confused and very disappointed
by the teacher and the system, receiving a failing grade at the
end of the semester.

I wanted to experience the joy of learning, not the
boredom of rote memorization. Even though these situations
happened a long time ago, the feelings were coming up with
other disappointments to be healed now.

The darkness of the past was bubbling up to be brought
into the light and released. I was shown by an inner vision,
that to grow, it is important to keep opening up, much like an
oyster that allows the grain of sand into its protected place.

The sand creates an irritation that eventually turns into a smooth, round and perfect pearl. I must allow these events into my life and not judge them as good or bad, right or wrong, then I may grow a beautiful pearl of wisdom and serenity.

When I was feeling vulnerable with so many grains of sand coming into my protected place, the support of my friends and guides told me that they came to me in unconditional love to support me in my growth to awareness in whatever capacity they could serve, in the oneness that we are.

The unexamined life is not worth living. — SOCRATES

Another visual that came to me was that of a large clock with a pendulum swinging back and forth. The still, perpendicular position represented balance, the pathway home. The swinging back and forth symbolized the choices I made, the complete circle of possibilities. I was mirroring and drawing events to me that guided me to the perpendicular path of stillness. I was still participating in the major swing back and forth, making my life confusing and upsetting. The experiences were lovingly pointed out to me to remember that I am the creator of my own life.

After sufficient introspection, it was time to move on and settle into the Texas lifestyle. My first apartment proved to be a convenient location for orientation to Austin, but soon the desire for a quieter, more peaceful place drew me to my second apartment located on a cascading, tree-filled hillside. One view was of the ever- changing colors of the desert valley.

I wanted to share my love of life with cats so, when I came across a dejected-looking Himalayan cat in a lighted, hot, glass cage, the last of a litter, I knew that I had found the first of my feline friends. Her facial pattern looked like someone had thrown a mud ball at her and it stuck. My first roommate whom I called, Shanti, Sanskrit for peace, moved into my apartment. Later, upon hearing of a breeder who had two Himalayan kittens left who would be sold as pets only, Kushi, Sanskrit for joy and happiness, joined us. Our family was complete.

Though I received a small monthly income from my divorce I needed a job to make ends meet. I was given a creative idea for a business, designing a protective, adult bib for silk blouses and men's ties. This idea was pursued as an outlet for my energy and as a means of, I thought, financial freedom.

To make a long story short, the cost of each bib was too high and my financial needs were not met. I donated the large, remaining inventory to a nursing home to brighten up the lives of the elderly population. Maybe this was the goal all along.

I didn't feel like a failure. It is the process that counts, not the goal. What I learned was invaluable. That I was capable, courageous, creative, and trusted myself to set up and complete this lesson: a negative success!

Part of letting go of my marriage and moving on involved relinquishing my first and last names. My father had died and Mom had remarried. There was no reason for any hard feelings because it was my free will choice. My new name was given to me, short and to the point: Leah Sean (Leah from my middle name Lee).

It was time to give attorneys a chance to redeem their reputations. Conferring with one about changing my name, he said it would take a week and cost $350. I drove directly to the courthouse. An hour later, at a cost of $50, I loved my

new name, felt good about my life, myself and my
discernment. Next time, I will skip the middle man.

Then I engaged in a real karmic event. An acquaintance
asked if I would invest some money in his company. If asked
such a question today, I would run the other way. The end
result was him driving off in a brand new car that I bought
for him.

The lesson apparently wasn't fully learned yet. I jumped
right into another situation of loaning money to a friend. His
business failed soon afterwards. He returned half of the
money, losing the other half and leaving me, in my naiveté,
with an audit.

It took awhile to release the energy from these
transactions, because at that time, I still thought of money as
my security. I learned that when something is being pointed
out to me in the form of a lesson, I was usually the last
to know.

I never understood this man's actions because what good
is obtaining money, if one has to undermine one's own
character to do so? Stealing from the one who pays you is like
having the goose who lays the golden egg for dinner.

This was the first time in my life that I had money at my
own disposal. I was feeling pretty cocky, though, not acting
wisely. I learned never to loan money to a man I was dating,
to never use money to bolster my ego and, next time, to think
twice before loaning money to anyone.

The lesson was invaluable and could not be learned in
school or by anyone's advice. This was strictly experiential.
The opportunity to try my wings was presented and I went
for it. The loss of this money and the resulting circumstances
that I created, I chalked up to paying my tuition.

We must see that nothing happens to us outside of our own choosing. The understanding and practice of this principle is the entire difference between a person who is the master of his life and one who sees himself as a victim of forces outside his control. — ALAN COHEN, THE HEALING OF THE PLANET EARTH: PERSONAL POWER AND PLANETARY TRANSFORMATION

When a spiritual conclave in Maui, Hawaii came to my attention, I was feeling so overwhelmed with being mindful of healing and letting go of old belief systems, I decided to attend.

The group was made up of a varied and interesting collection of people ranging from housewives to company executives. The first week we stayed in a motel-like setting, the second week in dorms, showering in outdoor booths open to the sky. Next to skinny dipping in a waterfall pond, showering in the outdoor booths took second place.

The most memorable and enjoyable experience occurred during the second week. One clear day with the sun shining against a brilliant, blue sky, we were invited to go swimming in a pool located halfway up the mountain. After driving for what seemed like an hour, we parked by a path that led us through an unwavering forest of tall bamboo trees on our way to a stream that cascaded down slippery, mossy, green rocks.

All of a sudden, a magnificent, multi-level waterfall forming a circular pool of inviting, cool water below, came into view. We had reached our destination.

Skinny dipping was the order of the day, bringing freedom to the rather shy adult. Moments later, naked as newborn babies, we jumped into the bubbly water, giggling with the delight of our newfound freedom. A Kahuna played his flute as its vibrations intertwined with the deep roar of the waterfall. No one noticed the nudity, only the natural joy of the freedom lost since childhood.

The two weeks over, a beach party was planned with dinner, served with ample amounts of Ecstasy, most of which was furnished by an executive from Houston. If this was how they had a good time together, I'd pass.

During one of the group leader's so-called sessions, a woman sitting on what was called the "hot seat" was being verbally degraded and brought to tears. She got up and ran out of the room, red-faced and embarrassed. At this point, my patience with such behavior ran out and my inner warrior came forth, asking to be the next one on the hot seat. My intention was to look into the facilitator's eyes and go inside to touch his soul, pointing out to him the stupidity and lack of compassion he was expressing. Upon receiving my mental message, he was shocked and ran out of the room.

I told the group leader that being a bully and insulting others was not behavior coming from enlightened beings. I found their activities to be very controlling, unloving and lacking in Divine Guidance. A few months after these meetings, the group broke up. After this confrontation, I escaped to be alone in the beauty and peace of the island on more than one occasion.

Happy to be back home in Austin, I started visiting a music/book store where I met the manager. The atmosphere was very restful and inviting. Five big soft recliners with head phones attached to the backs, made it comfortable to recline and listen to the music of your choice. Jim, the manager, introduced me to soft, spiritual music that I still listen to today. He also taught me to trust a good, loving hug which helped me drop the layer of protection I had built around myself. These invaluable gifts helped me to move on and learn to open my heart.

Each and every experience that came to me in the form of a lesson was healing and guided me on the path of self-awareness. I viewed these as blessings which I gratefully accepted.

I was about to meet a creative force within another human being that reflected myriad frequencies within myself. Douet, an artist friend who creates intuitive paintings of spirit and soul, was invited to my condo to hear a friend talk of our connections to self, others and the universe. Knowing that there was limited space in my living room, he still asked if his friend Vincent could attend. I quickly agreed after hearing Vincent's voice on the phone. We talked for two hours.

I opened the front door to see this handsome man with sparkling, blue eyes standing in front of me. I felt a connection, a belonging, a being in harmony with the energies that connected us on a soul level. We must have traveled these paths together many times before. After meeting we talked often on the phone, went out occasionally and enjoyed being in our own enclosed bubble, unaware of anyone else around us. Being an artist of high connections, Vincent, a professor of art at the University of Texas in Austin, has created spiritual sculpting, thought to be from the

time of Atlantis, and oil paintings that lift the viewer to a
higher level of consciousness and healing. Some day his gifts
will be more fully recognized for what they truly represent.

I woke up one morning knowing that it was time to move
on for the benefit of my path to enlightenment. I was not
consciously aware of how these times of knowing came into
my mind, just that to me knowing was a simple exercise in
faith and trust of the process. It just was. I felt like a snake
outgrowing its skin, shedding it and moving on to the next
great adventure.

Keeping myself open to guidance for the destination,
Seattle was mentioned three times in a week. Eager to know
if the area had the energy I was seeking, I flew there and fell
in love with the ocean and the whole setting: Mount Rainier,
Mount Baker, the San Juan Islands and the ever-so-charming
public market that displayed fresh fish, fruits and vegetables.
The decision was made. I would reside in the state
of Washington.

As a farewell, David and Ann took me to my favorite
oriental restaurant for dinner. I began to miss them already as
they said their good-byes. What a blessing it has been to live
near my two grown children as a single woman, making my
own choices in a close, uncomplicated way, allowing for a
deeper, more gratifying relationship with my grown son
and daughter.

Vincent invited me to brunch at a hotel known for its
sumptuous food and drink. Missing him was a given, but I
knew that to follow Spirit, I must flow with the guidance
that was being so generously offered toward furthering
my growth.

With help from friends and family, I packed a 12-foot
U-Haul, shedding unnecessary possessions. The next

morning, driving north into the wind blowing 50 miles an hour, the car struggled reaching only 45 miles per hour. Shanti and Kushi settled down and went to sleep.

Full of excitement, we arrived at our destination in Seattle to find that the apartment promised to us was no longer available. For a second, the excitement subsided and I almost felt sick. I knew there was a place somewhere nearby so I started searching the neighborhood streets looking for a rent sign. Sure enough, two blocks away there was an old, newly redecorated apartment available. We moved in.

3

Washington

The seed coat bursts through its outer layer revealing the latent potential

To create a sense of intimate participation with the universe and appreciate its deeper meaning, life will have to be recognized for the first time as a spiritual process. —THOMAS BERRY

Even moving into my new digs felt like a spiritual process with everything flowing so smoothly. The participation of the Divine is always there, in everything we experience, everyone we meet, connecting us always to the atonement that we are.

I unpacked and set out to explore the neighborhood on Capitol Hill, one of seven hills in Seattle, located about two miles north of downtown and two blocks from a neighborhood shopping area where there was a grocery store and two restaurants. This was one of the old sections of the city, but very clean and neighborhood safe.

The spicy aroma of Italian food coming from the corner restaurant reminded me that it was time for lunch, so I walked in. A handsome, dark-haired man named Peter greeted me, "We aren't open yet, but would you like a bowl of my homemade soup?" This cozy restaurant was to become a very nurturing place for me as I adjusted to my new life in the area.

With the ferry landing just down the hill from my apartment, I had easy access to the San Juan Islands where I visited often. Being a Midwest girl, living by the ocean opened new vistas never before available to me.

From the ferry, the islands looked like dollops of green, whipped cream floating around on a constantly-in-motion liquid dessert. Each island had its own rare and uncommon terrain. Orcas Island fascinated me the most. Driving up the curvy roads to the top, I looked through telescopes, revealing just how close the mountain was to the open ocean and to Canada. It felt like going to the ends of the Earth, peeking over and finding more where there seemed to be no more. What a strange feeling!

Two months after arriving in Seattle, I drove east over the mountains to stay in a cabin that I had reserved for two nights, giving me time for rest and recuperation from the move. On the drive over, close to the top of the mountain, I was suddenly enveloped in a white, sun-filled mist. Momentarily, everything seemed to stand still, like there was no time, freeing my mind for these words to come to me.

It is as though we are being readied for rebirth.
The soft, cool fog being the womb.
Separating, yet joining us as one.
Surrounding and protecting us during the gestation period.
For we the meek to rise up
and inherit the Earth.

I arrived at this cozy cabin nestled in the pine trees, unpacked and set out to explore the lodge and have dinner. I ate quickly and returned to the cabin, anxious to luxuriate in the private hot tub on my cabin deck. Large, feathery snowflakes started floating down as I stepped into the comforting, steamy water. The awareness of the pine trees, so great in stature and height, maybe six stories high, brought the realization that they must have viewed history from the beginning of life on the Earth.

Coming out of a white background, separate and unique flakes fell first through the steam then into the tub, melting on impact. The snowflakes seemed to come out of one, separating, coming to the Earth then melting and evaporating, returning to the source. This same symbolism kept appearing to me through different mediums, reminding me of my temporary place on this Earth before I, once again, become one.

The two days at the cabin went by very quickly, almost like I had been transported to another dimension, creating an atmosphere that allowed me to feel safe enough to let go into my higher self.

As the balance of inner knowing and wisdom are brought
forth into the conscious awareness of the illusion,
how strange and alone one feels in this physical world.
As the peace, love and atonement are experienced,
out of the dream,
I see that fear has no power.
The dream no longer holds its illusion as reality.

In this space I was reminded to be a joyful child, to let go, to be guided and to fulfill my purpose for being here on Earth. To do it with love and Divine Guidance, breaking the consciousness of belief systems that bespeak of pain and struggle.

To see my authentic self is to
finally be free.
To live that freedom is
"be-ing" in action.

My soul was bursting at the seams to come forth and express itself fully, bringing lasting peace and happiness to myself and then radiating it out into the world. I was told not to look beyond myself for the truth, for it was within me, waiting to be remembered. I felt so euphoric that staying in my body was almost impossible. To share this experience and feeling with others, it was necessary to stay grounded, so on the return from this enlightening journey, I saw a job looming in the near future.

We serve each other most powerfully simply by
finding our own place. — AUTHOR UNKNOWN

Going back into the job market brought me to the experiences of selling Chinese herbs; demonstrating and selling a new tartar sauce in grocery stores and wineries; renting videos; working temp services; and filling in for a few days here and there for friends who owned stores, while they were on vacation.

My life was filled with possibilities that I knew were not facts or truth, maybe more like sparks of inspiration. I was eager to explore and experience whatever came to me in finding my own way. In this belief, I encountered what we call painful situations along the way, but as the French say, "Pain is the craft entering into the apprentice." Now I was grounded.

A few months after arriving at my new apartment, an inner voice suggested that I drive up Mount Rainier. It was getting late, but I always trust my inner guidance and knew

there was a reason to go. After the long drive up the
mountain, I went inside the observatory hoping to become
aware of my reason for being there. Viewing the magnificent,
snow-capped top amidst the gray, angular rocks, I marveled
at the miracle of life and nature. The meeting of two
phenomena, a lava flow and an Earth shift that created a
dichotomy, one side angular and the other rounded and soft,
much like the symbolism of male and female.

The sun was setting and nothing of note was happening
so I headed down the mountain. Again, I heard a voice in my
head saying to stop at one of the pull-outs. I looked back up
at the mountain against the darkening sky and saw several
flying disks, easily visible, shooting out of the top. It was awe
inspiring. Unfortunately, they disappeared as fast as they had
appeared, leaving lenticular clouds, rounded with smooth
edges still in place even though there was a sturdy wind
blowing. My purpose fulfilled, I drove home. Step by step,
I was guided to remember who I am and my connection to
everyone, everything and all.

One fall weekend, I drove down the Oregon coastline to
stay at a resort boasting cabins perched on a cliff overlooking
the ocean. The first night I sat on a bench outside my cabin,
listening to the thunderous roar of the surf, watching the
sun set. At these times of being in a peaceful space, my higher
self brings forth beautiful pictoral poems.

The surf is roaring so loudly that it shuts out any other
noises, allowing my mind to wander.
How fast everything changes,
reminding me that to truly experience life,
I must stay in the present, for there is no other time.
The vibrant sun is a half circle partially hidden by the
clouds, sinking fast just above the skyline.
There is such a peacefulness in the resignation of the ending
of another day.
Would that we could be so peaceful and
accepting while just being.

I was to see my mother for the last time when she visited
me in Washington. Most of my life I was willing to go along
with her unreasonable demands, but after leaving my
marriage, it was time to pay attention to my own life and let
go of past, dysfunctional behavior. Even though we hadn't
seen each other for quite awhile, it was apparent that nothing
had changed with her. I told her that whatever she did to be
happy made me happy for her, unless it meant interfering in
my life and choices.

The years of frustration and wanting her to love me came
into focus. All of a sudden, there was a place of knowing.
Since she didn't love herself, she wasn't capable of loving
anyone else. For the first time in this life, I was free from
seeking love from my mother and started loving myself. Our
love for each other was very strong, but our needs and
insecurities got in the way of our friendship. Now there was a
completion, and I felt the part of my body that held this
sadness leave forever.

> *What lies behind us and what lies before us are*
> *tiny matters compared to what lies within us.* —
> RALPH WALDO EMERSON

The water fountain located in the center of Edmonds, a town north of Seattle, was the front yard of my next apartment which was located over a store. I often walked the loop around town ending up at the beach to watch the magnificent sunset with other town's people. Waiting for the sun to set, I closed my eyes, allowing me to focus on my listening. It is amazing how much we miss by being so distracted by what we see. The seagulls chatted while the ferry's foghorns vibrated their presence. I felt at one with the sounds, free from visual distraction.

One day while reading, all of a sudden, I felt light-headed as I left my conscious mind. I was no longer present. I don't remember seeing anything, just having a very strong feeling of peace as a soft voice told me, "Don't make it so hard." My consciousness then shifted back to my book. So many gifts in the form of these experiences came to me while living in the Seattle area that have connected me more to my soul essence.

Starting to feel antsy and not knowing what to do, I planned a trip to Mexico. The living expenses were low, the country was very beautiful and I had always liked the Mexican people. A perfect, new adventure!

Texas was my stop-over place on the way to Mexico, so I briefly visited my daughter Ann. She opened her home to me, but my visit quickly became intrusive in the eyes of her boyfriend.

Coming to my rescue were the Douets, old friends from living in Austin when I first left my marriage. They offered me a bed for awhile in their home. It all felt right, knowing that a time would arrive when there would be a knowing to move on. During one of our tea breaks, resting and philosophizing about the meaning of life and our part in it,

Dawn, being very psychic, saw me living in New Mexico, not Mexico.

By this time, my son David, also a free spirit and yet unmarried, decided to move from Seattle to New Mexico, resulting in his driving to Austin to pick me up. We headed north, living for awhile in Albuquerque. Then Kushi and I prepared to move to Taos, our first choice of a place to live. Shanti had found new companions to share her life with.

New Mexico

The seed pushes through the top soil strong and resolute, growing toward a source of radiated energy

Finally, all we can do is let the days instruct us.
Knowing that the only gift worth having is the grace
To go on with the job to be done.
There is no holding on in this world.
We came to this extraordinary place.
Let us lead extraordinary lives.
— I DREAMED OF AFRICA. DIRECTOR HUGH HUDSON,
COLUMBIA/TRI-STAR STUDIOS, 2000

On my journey, I felt uncomfortable when pushed to go outside of my normal behavior, that of an independent loaner. Barely existing from month to month on my small income from alimony, it was necessary to share a living space until my next job in Taos. My desire in my middle age years was to be financially independent. I was out of my comfort zone, but knew on a spiritual level that this lesson was a reminder that we are all on this journey together. In retrospect, those were the times that I learned the most about leading an extraordinary life from the loving gifts bestowed upon me from otherwise unexplored experiences.

Once pushed beyond my comfort zone, I explored other avenues toward knowing self. For a very short time, I shared an apartment in Albuquerque while looking for a job. There was no job to be found and the energy in Albuquerque and the lifestyle were not to my liking, especially on a soul level.

I was so excited about exploring Taos and looking for a job that the loud snoring on the bus trip there didn't bother me as I observed the splendid beauty of the desert, the mountains and the gushing stream following the highway.

The historic La Fonda Hotel, located on the downtown plaza, was happy to send a car to pick me up, especially since it was off-season. I had only $90 to cover food and lodging for two days and two nights. Some very creative money management was needed. After talking to the managers at each hotel, my room rates dropped considerably, especially after agreeing to stay in the less desirable rooms. The downtown hotel proved to be very noisy at night, so I was delighted to stay at the Mable Dodge House in a room that boasted a view of a sacred cross standing not far from my window, a place where many spiritual ceremonies took place, or so I was told.

The next morning, after a very generous, free breakfast, I ventured forth to the interview I had set up at the San Geronimo Lodge before coming to Taos. With no form of transportation available, I walked 5 miles to each interview. Needless to say, I arrived a little sweaty but very determined. The second day they gave me good news: I was hired. This supported and pointed out that my trust of stepping outside myself and going for it was fulfilled and satisfied. My job was as a front desk clerk which consisted of answering the phone, taking reservations, and checking the guests in.

The reason for meeting two artists who owned a home three blocks from the lodge was revealed to me when I saw their adorable, adobe guest house that, at the time, was occupied. On an intuitive level, I saw myself living there in a few months. This was a good omen. Stubbornness and desire do give one the will to go forward, and I had plenty of both, knowing that there is nothing my mind can conceive of that I cannot have.

Getting on the bus to return to Albuquerque, I had a job but no place to live. I was given the name of a lady who owned a condo in Taos and was looking for a single, older woman who would take care of her strikingly beautiful space that had skylights, an adobe fireplace and a large bedroom with a brass bed. A week later, with my son David's help, I moved into a new, furnished condo with no money. The agreement was to pay rent at the end of the first month, in the middle of the second month and on the first of the month thereafter. I did.

Letting the day instruct me, I flowed with what was, accepting the outcome. I moved on with grace toward the job to be done, accepting with gratitude the profound gifts that were bestowed upon me. I was living an extraordinary life in this remarkable place.

Courage and willingness, not money, brought me to a place of living with grace and in grand abundance, anyway, the abundance that really counts. Only true abundance nourishes our heart and soul. Financial abundance, although necessary for rent, food and miscellaneous items, maintains our physical body temple or our work vehicle.

There were only 17 rooms at the lodge which were not enough to keep me busy, so I took on such chores as baking, preparing breakfast and cleaning the lobby although those duties may have been there all along. As a bed and breakfast lodge, the manager, cleaning ladies and I prepared and served the breakfast, followed by a bonding time of washing dishes and cleaning up. Knowing how hard the cleaning ladies worked and hearing about their challenges in life, I learned even more about courage, reminding me of a thought that flowed through me one day, that, those who have suffered the most, express more profoundly their humanity.

Walking to work and the grocery store was good and healthy exercise, but enough was enough. The day after I wished for a bicycle, my neighbor told me about a used one for sale in a nearby store. I walked into the shop and saw a beautiful, blue bicycle called Free Spirit for only $50 and knew that it was meant to be mine!

The ride to the lodge, located on an uphill, three mile road, left me exhilarated and sweaty at six a.m. But at five in the evening my desire to be the free spirit that I am, and to feel the wind blowing through my hair, was realized as coasted all the way home. What a rush!

After working at the lodge for almost a year, I became aware that the manager was abusing drugs and alcohol. Some days he would come in looking very disheveled, acting moody and abrupt with the guests. When they began to ask if I was the manager/owner I knew my job was coming to an end. I was right. On New Year's Eve, he handed me my check and fired me. Thanking him for making it possible for me to stay in Taos, he started to cry as he walked back to the music room. I followed, offering him a hug, saying thank you and no hard feelings. His next comment, that he hoped to be as

spiritually awake as I was, surprised me. Had I reacted to
being fired, instead of appreciating having been hired in the
first place, I would never have known the truth of his deepest
feelings.

Shortly after I was fired, the owner sold the lodge to an
alcoholic recovery group. In truth, the manager was very
good to us as his employees. It felt like he was, like me at
times, hiding from the truth and running away from taking a
good honest look at himself.

With a gap between this job and the next, I was again at
the place of creative money management. I have always made
it a practice to pay bills on the first of the month, living on
whatever is left over. This leaves me with a clear conscience,
but sometimes the food pickings are pretty small. At one of
these times, I asked my guides what to do and very clearly
heard a man's voice ask, "Have you ever gone hungry?"
I looked down at my rather rounded body and answered,
"Do I look hungry?" I burst out laughing, the answer was, no.

> *Beloved Mother, Father, I accept with gratitude*
> *your guidance in helping me focus on the right*
> *path that will encourage my soul to grow into the*
> *specific splendor you intended when you first*
> *planted it as a seed in your garden.*
> — AUTHOR UNKNOWN

A friend from Seattle came to visit and generously offered
me one of her backpacks to carry groceries. A neighbor
offered me her abundance of fresh vegetables which I learned
to accept with humility and gratefulness. Having no extra
money, yet living in good fortune, again taught me the true
meaning of abundance and kept me in the ever-present now.

A friend who owned a spiritual book store asked me to work for her during the grieving process from the loss of her significant other. Merlin's Garden gave me the opportunity to come into the presence of souls who brought up powerful emotions of recognition from other lifetimes together. The money was a blessing, but the souls I met were priceless.

People from all over the world came in to browse, even travelers from space and time who acknowledged themselves with a look, a feel of their energy or a statement of their purpose on Earth.

One day at work, four books displayed standing up on a table fell on the floor with a loud thud for no apparent reason. As I leaned over to put them back on the table, I was shocked to see that their titles were arranged in such a way that gave me an answer to a question I had posed earlier. Later my friend told me that her deceased partner was still present in the store. Now there was a more meaningful understanding of other instances that had occurred, like seeing someone out of the corner of my eye, hearing voices and seeing items being moved. The high level of energy present in the store created a space where physical and spiritual could meet. This job ended when my friend had worked through the grief from her loss, and was able to come back to work.

It seems that I was continually looking for a job and a place to rent. I kept reminding myself that I chose my path while in spirit form for a reason, so I just kept putting one foot in front of the other.

With no other job opportunities in sight, a psychic friend suggested that I tent on some land she owned north of Questa, a hot, sandy desert with no trees. This offer, coming out of the blue, felt like guidance, a gift to live outdoors and spend time with my dear cat friend, Kushi.

David bought and set up a six by seven foot tent, placing straw and a canvas tarp on the ground to make it softer and dryer inside. I moved in with my bed mat and a steamer trunk that had belonged to my mother where I stored my clothes and a few belongings. Had I known the events that I was going to participate in and observe, there would have been no way to keep me in my body from the elation of the spiritual adventure.

A friend helped me build an L-shaped wall to shield the kitchen and shower area from the wind which blew almost all of the time. All water had to be carried in for drinking and cooking, sometimes retrieving water from a nearby mountain stream for the sun shower. Kushi and I were living in the middle of the desert with wolves, mountain lions, bears, severe wind and rain storms and dust in our food, yet we felt very safe with an overpowering love. This wasn't a very comfortable way for my dear cat to live but, in spite of it all, she cuddled up at night and went to sleep.

> *The more difficult the journey, the deeper the depths of purification.* — BUDDHA

Later David's housing was disrupted in the middle of tourist season, so he bought a tent and moved down the hill from us with his cat, Puff. At night, in total darkness, lit only by a single lantern, we were provided the space and time to philosophize about our chosen paths in this life.

In the purity of silence, communing with nature, away from all intrusions and distractions, I became the observer, standing outside of myself. Insight of purpose emerged, connecting us spiritually on a level never before possible.

My journey had been filled with the richness and blessings of having a kindred spirit, reminding me that we were family in both form and spirit. Most people living in the illusion of the third dimension saw us as mother and son. I saw a fellow traveler. Those who were unable to see beyond the physical body temple had little or no understanding of such a Divine Blessing.

The dark nights, the sky ablaze with stars, allowed the viewing of UFOs. One night I saw a glowing, cigar-shaped vehicle which turned, revealing itself to be a disc disappearing into Ute Mountain. Air Force jets flying low in and around the mountain the next morning confirmed that I had, indeed, seen a UFO.

A few days later I went across the highway to meet with Drunvalo Melchisedeck, a friend of Vincent's. He took time to talk even though he and his family were packing to move to Texas. He related to me that Ute Mountain was being used as a landing place on Earth for the ships from Sirius, star of the constellation Canis Major, the brightest star in the heavens, also called the Dog Star. Drunvalo said that rattle snakes had been seeded on the mountain to keep out any intruders. I will never know since the intended warning was enough for me.

After seeing the UFO, lofty events and dreams started coming into my life. In an awake dream, I was in a tall building going up in an elevator. When I reached the top floor, the elevator continued to ascend higher up into the sky. When it started to fall back toward the Earth's gravity, a ledge appeared which I grabbed onto, seeing a window that extended the width of the ledge behind it. I was asked the question, "Do you want to go through the window?" Suddenly an opening appeared, and I saw beings milling around on the other side. The dream ended abruptly as

I woke up. It seemed they were giving me the choice to leave. Either I said no, or it wasn't my time yet. I will probably never know.

One night while in bed but not yet asleep, a brilliant light so bright that it bothered even my closed eyes, went right through me, much like an x-ray. I don't remember anything else, but after that, my dreams became very vivid, filling my thoughts with spiritually connected ideas about who we are and why we are here. Swirling clouds of pink, blue and purple would appear out of nowhere, passing across the sky. At times, I saw cloud angels that stayed in one place in spite of strong winds which moved the other puffy, floating clouds.

Whatever happened, I never felt the same again. Maybe I was seeing what had always been there.

Nothing real can be threatened. Nothing unreal exists. Herein lies the peace of God.
— AUTHOR UNKNOWN

The neighbors said that winter in this valley could have temperatures of 30 to 40 degrees below zero, so it was time to move out of the tent and look for another job. Going from job to job, always starting anew seemed a little erratic, but to quote Pablo Picasso:

Every act of Creation is, first of all, an act of Destruction. — PABLO PICASSO

A guest house located outside Taos on a magnificent plateau was available to a single, middle-aged woman. Again, age and gender paid off!

My next job was as a hostess in a popular restaurant located on the slopes of the Taos Ski Valley. There were celebrities who did their best to remain anonymous, like

Lloyd Bridges, and those who didn't mind being recognized, like one of my old favorites, Tab Hunter. The season was over quickly and I needed to expand my job search. I bought an old, blue station wagon with the money earned from working at the lodge. After a month and no job in Taos, it was time to consider moving. I had a car and didn't know where to move. David wanted to move to Arkansas but had no car. We packed a U-Haul and headed for eastern Arkansas.

I felt like a caterpillar in the cocoon state, releasing the beautiful butterfly, an ancient symbol of the Spirit.

Arkansas

The sun and rain nourish the delicate green shoots that now grow strong, expanding and reaching

The green shoots nourished by the sun and the rain grow strong with the knowledge that, before a seed can burst forth through the soil, it must set up a solid root system, a foundation that grounds it firmly in the physical world to discover what it is meant to be. And so it is for us.

Even though proof of competence as a soul may not yet be fully recognized, I serve from the capacity of what I already know. For now, my truths are based on the here and now.

In the awareness that truths are revealed in contradiction, my stubborn convictions guided me to continue following my own path with no more expectations or explanations. Every lesson to be learned in a lifetime also brings forth a gift to share with others. By placing myself in direct participation with the events that were shown to me, others were also benefiting. This thought gave me the courage and desire to move through whatever was given to me in love by my higher self and others working so diligently on the other side of the veil.

I checked out two towns before I decided to move to Eureka Springs, an area I had thought about moving to after Texas. Driving through the downtown area, I spotted and welcomed a help wanted sign in a hotel window. The manager hired me on the spot, and I set out to find a place to live even though the choices were limited because of high tourist season.

The first apartment I looked at was located in the basement of a house owned by a practicing, black witch. The second, which I chose, was a log cabin located on two acres of an estate, 15 miles from Eureka Springs. What a peaceful setting, allowing me my precious freedom!

About six months later when David decided to return to Nebraska, a friend told me about a three-story, historical house located five blocks from work. I moved, saved on gas, walked to work and called this place home until moving to Arizona two years later.

In the time that I worked at the hotel as front desk clerk, it brought me great pleasure to meet and have time to philosophize with our guests from all over the world, who were also seeking the answer to "who am I?" These people from other cultures, other countries, of different races, colors and creeds, came to the same conclusion: we are all one. To reiterate, we are each separate expressions, unique in our points of view and backgrounds, but ultimately all one. The more I moved around the country and the more people who came into my life, the more this truth became obvious to me.

The job of front desk clerk also placed me in the position of hostess, not only for the hotel but the whole area. Recommendations given to our guests were: the Blue Springs where the Navajo Indians stopped on the government-forced march called the Trail of Tears in 1830; the unique, architectural design of the Thorn Crown glass chapel where my son David would soon be married; the local springs that were first discovered by a doctor who was hunting in the area in the late 1800s, drawing many people there for healing; and the yearly Blues Fest that brought in musicians who entertained in the streets, in the bars and lobbies of the hotels. I also recommended restaurants to our guests, my favorite being The Autumn Breeze, owned by my friend Richard who specialized in coconut shrimp.

There was so much more, but this is not a travel guide. I was thankful for the people who had given me the richness and deeper understanding of life and self also for the beautiful, engaging places that have set the background for these gifts.

One day I answered the phone expecting to take a reservation, and heard my daughter Ann's voice announcing her marriage in December. She sounded so excited that I could only be happy for her. The manager gave me a week of paid vacation and Kushi and I were off to Austin, Texas to witness the joining of two families.

There were a few minor incidents, driving 80 miles an hour through Dallas, but we arrived safely at the motel where Ann had made reservations for all of the guests. After reunions and a restful night's sleep, I woke up to the realization that my hanging clothes bag was still in Arkansas. A hurried call to my friend back home and my things arrived

by express mail the next day. It was very helpful to have
understanding friends after a brain lapse.

My daughter, who used to play in the backyard tree house
and who helped me bake cookies at Christmas, now stood
before me as a beautiful bride about to embark on a new life
with her groom. Friends and family gathered for the
ceremony and reception in an old mansion of grandeur,
resplendent of the early 1900s. The rice was thrown and the
party ended with congratulations to the bride and groom.
I was delighted that Ann thought so much of her new in-laws
and they of her. I was often reminded of how fortunate I am.
This was one of those times.

Working at the hotel introduced me to a lifestyle that was
totally foreign to the one I had chosen. I was the one out of
step, the outsider in this setting and among the people who
hung out there. The hotel had a reputation for being a place
of wine, women and song to such an extent that it was
difficult for me to understand. But I am thankful for the
canvas of all possibilities provided for my learning,
discernment and remembering compassion. Again, I walked
my own path.

One day, after working there for two and a half years, it all
blew up and the manager fired me. As I walked out the door
in the middle of the day, I felt so free! Working there had
nothing to do with love of the job and everything to do with
fear of not having money. The manager gave me the gift of
forcing this belief to come to an end.

Not being financially independent yet, as fall changed into
winter, there were no jobs to be found. Even the full-time
positions were cut to part-time, with some businesses closing
altogether until spring. In my life, I had earned a degree in

compassion and the desire to help others, so I sent for credentials giving me the authority to perform weddings.

I wrote two marriage ceremonies, one for heterosexuals and the other for gay couples who, as far as I am concerned, have the same right to sanction their love. Two robes were made, cards were printed and distributed to lodges and hotels and one month later I performed a marriage which was to be the one and only before moving to Sedona, Arizona.

The following winter I had plenty of time to look within. It was the longest, most depressing period of time since leaving my marriage. When Eureka was in off season it literally became a ghost town. My friends had enough money to move to warmer climates until spring. There was more snow and ice than usual, and I barely had enough money to pay my bills and still eat. It was a very long, dark, cold winter, and I felt very alone. As I thought about the word *alone*, an "aha" came to me, that it also means *all one*. This brought into focus the dichotomy of the word and the true perception of its real truth. In losing everything, I had space to gain everything.

> *One may chase after a butterfly only to have it elude you. But, if you sit quietly, it may land upon your hand.* — AUTHOR UNKNOWN

Boy, did I ever sit quietly waiting for the butterfly, not knowing then what a profound gift was coming my way. The circumstances may not have been to my liking nor would I have chosen them, but my beloved guides always bring to me the appropriate situations to learn and grow. There was one source of heat, a very old gas stove unit located in one of the five small rooms where Kushi and moved our bedding and spent the winter months.

In crisis, I learned that we were not alone. This was a big step for me, as I was very stubborn and hell bent on making it on my own. A quantum shift took place and my demeanor went from I'd rather do it myself to yes, I need help.

Connie and her husband Tom, who is more like a brother to me, offered short-term financial assistance in my time of need. The offer had been made before, but at that time being determined to learn true abundance, which has nothing to do with money, I had turned down their offer. I bless them both for their love, friendship and ability and willingness to share at this time and gratefully accepted their offer. Being both teacher and student, we also had each other to love and support our growth to awareness. Not in doing it for each other, but in lovingly supporting one another in our process of awakening. In addition to their practical help, my sister's words comforted me.

Letting Go
There is a place in life for endings
A time for letting go
A stopping of activity,
An interruption in the flow of life
That surges all around.
It's in this quiet space
New blessings can be found.
— CONNIE HUNT, LISTENING, AN INNER JOURNEY, 1986A

Here is another one of her poems that I value reflecting on.

The Greatest Gift

The gift is your heart
That you may care.
The gift is your time
That you may share.
The gift of your hand
Stretched out to another.
The gift is your life
As friend and lover.
For the greatest gift
We have to give
Is just ourselves
And the way we live.

— CONNIE HUNT, REACHING, 2ND EDITION, 1983

I have been told that it is not necessary to understand life, but it is necessary to live it without fear. It is also necessary to go through the dark in order to live in the light. Being alone, without a job, little money, friends out of town, I moved into the dark night of the soul, a psychological bottom. My shift in identity from ego to soul's expression felt like I was reaching down into my throat with my hand, pulling out my gut level pain and dysfunctional identification with the false self by asking, "If I am not who I have been told that I am or thought myself to be, then who am I?" I can continue to project my dysfunctional behavior on others, both at their expense if they allow it and at my expense if I stay stuck in ego.

My ever-loving guides gave me the following:

The Shadow Of Me

I turned to look and saw my shadow,
a curious part of this being called I.
What could this be, a separate expression and
so similar to me, yet, always apart.
All of a sudden, I realized that the shadow
was more me than I.
What I was seeking was the true expression
of me in this body temple.
How to bring the two together as one?
In my seeking a completeness, the insight that I had only
to accept, flow and be open for the integration of
who I am and who I thought myself to be.
Finally being at one, one with all
and not knowing who I am.

As I look back now, I see just how masterful and powerful my dear and loving friend Kushi was as she cuddled and communicated with me during this time. I depended on her more than I realized and gratefully accepted the healing her presence offered. My higher self, always available to assist, gave me:

You have to be to do.
You don't have to do to be.

This simple but very wise perspective on life has and continues to give me great comfort. We all receive guidance from a higher power whether we are aware of it or not. Some call it intuition, a feeling, a knowing. We are not alone.

Would I have chosen these lessons from my ego-driven will? No! Even though it was painful at times, when I let go, it flowed. When I stubbornly held on, it resisted. My strong will relented, feeling the emotions and allowing the tightness in my body to flow from me. Holding on and resisting this process would have held me in bondage to the feelings stored in body, mind and spirit.

Our bodies may be compared to an onion with layer after layer of old, stored emotions, even from other lifetimes. When we release a layer, it is possible to move on to the next and the next, until we are free from emotions that are keeping us from being the bright and shiny being that is our true expression.

> *All experiences of imbalance which have taken place on the Earth so far ... all the emotions around them have been necessary to bring the will and Spirit to a place of being ready and able to balance with one another freely. The will needs to be allowed to express all of its fears and other emotions, then it can clearly receive the Spirit's guidance. The Spirit needs to accept and receive this emotional expression also so that it knows what its own manifested part is experiencing. —* CEANNE DEROHAN, RIGHT USE OF WILL: HEALING & EVOLVING THE EMOTIONAL BODY

Finally spring came, my friends returned to their jobs and life went on. One day I received a call from David telling me that he and his fiancée were getting married in June, in the Thorn Crown Chapel in Eureka. Having lived in this area for over two years, I knew of the nicer places available for the prenuptials and reception. I reserved accommodations for the out-of-town guests and the wedding chapel, ordered the cake and arranged for gourmet eats at the reception.

When June arrived, family and friends came to witness the ceremony and the love shared by David and his bride. They were both dressed in white with the background of the sun shining in through the glass panels, creating a magical setting. After the wedding, with the loving support of family and friends they moved to Sedona, Arizona to live and share their lives as man and wife. I had planned to move to North Carolina at this time but at David's request I moved to Arizona to become acquainted with his new wife and beautiful daughter, Miranda.

Miranda and I enjoyed going horse back riding and out to lunch, especially Taco Bell, her favorite at that time. I even slept on the lower bunk of her bed for two months while waiting for my house to be built. My time spent with Miranda was filled with playfulness on our morning walks and the pleasure and wonder about having such an intelligent, sweet granddaughter.

Later, when their son Joshua was born, I found great joy in having him stay overnight, preparing his favorite meal of macaroni and cheese, then playing with his all time favorite match box cars. I was amazed at his presence and willingness to be away from his parents at such a young age.

As I was preparing to move on, a fierce independence burst forth as if it had been standing by waiting to be recognized. I knew that a large part of the energy that was bringing my gifts into the physical world came from the joy of being a detached loner. I loved deeply but was aware that, when I truly loved another, there was a willingness to let go of him and honor his soul's place in the world. I had set myself on a course of living where detachment was a natural state of being.

I asked my guides and higher self why these feelings were coming up now, after the wedding. My understanding was that David and I had just completed a part of our agreement in this life. Time for celebration! That, although there would be times when we would feel apart, we would fulfill other aspects of our souls contracts. Had I been furnished with wings, I would have flown with joy!

Feeling quite vulnerable, like a newborn baby, my choices were to either be with new friends who didn't know and expect the same responses as the old me or to be alone. In the transition from "acting in order to be lovable" to "growing into the natural child, the real self," there was never an intent to shun my family and friends. I was just asking them to love me enough to allow the space and time I needed for the affirmation of my own soul's expression.

The following partial quote, taken out of context from Gary Cooper's character in the conclusion of the movie *The Fountainhead* (from the book and the screenplay written by Ayn Rand), is not meant to be harsh but it states very clearly my truth.

> *His truth was his only motive. He went ahead*
> *whether others agreed with him or not. His*
> *integrity was his only banner. He served no one.*
> *He must think and act on his own. His mind*
> *cannot work under any form of compulsion or*
> *subjected to the needs and desires of others. The*
> *terms are the right to exist for one's own sake.*

Standing outside societal and parental programming, my true soul's expression emerged. Now I was an observer and contributor to the process of an authentic state of being. I relate to you the loving guidance that has been given to me along the way, although living in this manner takes a willingness to surrender with the practice of being mindful.

In a Christopher Columbus movie I saw years ago, I felt at one with the following message:

> *Nothing that results from human progress is achieved with unanimous consent. Those who are enlightened before the others are condemned to pursue that light in spite of others.*

I stand in the center of my being, taking back my power with no apologies for who I am. I am overflowing with unconditional love and compassion and easily brought to tears in the presence of pain and suffering. I am that I am, a luminous being knowing that, by expressing who I am, the vibrations and consciousness of humanity will be raised forever. True spirituality is peaceful, nonintrusive, gentle, compassionate, humble and quiet.

> *The props assist the house*
> *Until the house is built,*
> *And then the props withdraw -*
> *And adequate, erect,*
> *The house supports itself,*
> *Ceasing to recollect*
> *The auger and the carpenter.*
> *Just such a retrospect*
> *Hath the perfected life,*
> *A past of plank and nail.*
> *And slowness, - then the scaffolds drop -*
> *Affirming it a soul.*
> — EMILY DICKINSON, COMPLETE POEMS, PART FIVE:
> THE SINGLE HOUND, XXVI

Sedona

Setting deep roots into Mother Earth, growing toward the Sun of God

Like the Semitic nomads, we live in a desert with many lonely travelers who are looking for a moment of peace, for a fresh drink and for a sign of encouragement so that they can continue their mysterious search for freedom. — HENRI J. M. NOUWEN, THE WOUNDED HEALER

The following summer I continued on my search for freedom by packing my few possessions in the back of my pick-up truck, with the help of a friend who worked at the hotel. My former boss offered Kushi and me a luxurious air-conditioned room with a double Jacuzzi tub for our last night's stay in Eureka, a loving and generous gift. My traveling companion was happy to be in a cool, comfortable spot, so she curled up and went to sleep. Staying at the hotel gave me the opportunity to say good-bye to my fellow workers.

At three the next morning after only four hours of sleep, I packed my overnight bag, put Kushi in the truck and we were off. There was no air-conditioning in my truck so starting early was a good idea, especially in July. I found out why Kushi had been acting unusually agitated when I noticed her frequent urination with blood in it. A full-fledged bladder infection! Not knowing what to do, I headed toward Sedona to find a vet.

Although we stopped once to rest, it was so hot and poor Kushi was so miserable that I decided to drive straight through from Arkansas to Arizona. Driving at night was cool but a little troubling as the gas tank was about empty. At this early hour, we found nothing open. It was three o clock in the morning, and I was running on fumes so I asked my guardian angel for guidance. The stars were ablaze in the night sky as we drove on and, lo and behold, over the next big hill appeared the bright lights announcing a gas station.
As I pulled in to fill up, I met a couple who was also running on empty, also elated almost kissing the attendant. Feeling much better, I drove on with renewed energy. Always ask and you will, indeed, receive.

Upon arrival in Sedona, my first thought was to find a veterinarian. One hundred and forty dollars later, Kushi had been hydrated and given antibiotics for the infection. Although I prefer holistic treatment, I was exhausted and Kushi was desperate, hence our willingness to accept help from a traditional vet.

Looking for a place to stay for one night, I encountered the same response that had plagued us on all of our moves, no cats allowed. After many inquiries, someone recommended the airport mesa. It was very expensive but did allow cats. The hot shower and good food felt heavenly after forcing myself to stay awake for two and a half days. It took awhile to settle down, but we finally went to sleep.

I had contacted a friend of my sister who rents short-term condos in the Village of Oak Creek, where I stayed for the next six weeks while looking for a longer term place to live. My new daughter-in-law returned to Nebraska to sell her home, so David was also at loose ends with no place to stay. Since there were two bedrooms located on either side of a large living room, David bunked in the second bedroom until he found a charming house located on a high ridge overlooking the Mingus Mountains. I finally found and temporarily settled into a small trailer that had gorgeous, red rock views located two miles south of Sedona.

Following through on Kushi's bladder problem, I contacted a holistic vet who recommended giving her colloidal silver. Asking where it was available, she guided me to an herb store where the owner not only sold me the product, but offered me a two-day-a-week job. This was perfect. Now to find a place to live that was closer to work.

I was told about a one-room apartment available just one mile from work. The rent seemed very high for a small bedroom, walk-in closet and small bath. The selling point was a 25 by 15 foot second-story deck that gave a panoramic view of Sedona's vibrant, magnificent, red rocks. Guidance was always right there in my face, if I paid attention and listened.

I learned a lot about herbs, again, meeting people from all over the world as I explored Sedona. About five months after starting to work at the store, the atmosphere shifted from friendly to control mode. New, unrealistic duties were added to my daily routine. But, after all, it was her store and business could be conducted according to her desires. A phrase given to me again by my guides was, "Don't take your body anywhere your soul doesn't want to be." My soul didn't want to be there anymore, so I told her I quit and she said, "You're fired."

After that I stayed in Sedona for another six months which left me time to walk, sleep and meditate. Experiences long forgotten were coming into my conscious mind. There must be a purpose, one that can be understood in my present state of knowing. The question came up, How can I live as who I am in the Earth consciousness as it exists now and still be true to myself? With an interruption of the easy flow of energy, I stopped for a period of time, allowed, remained open, focused on the moment at hand and, with patience, waited to be guided.

On long walks as I released my conscious thoughts allowing my state of mind to be open and receptive, words and thoughts were channeled through me. I share my higher selfs wisdom with you now.

There was a finer line now between the freedom of dreams and illusion of wakefulness. Neither was fully aware, both wandering, passing through each experience hardly conscious of what had transpired. The separation of yesterday and tomorrow fades into the ever-present now. My perceptions of reality seemed to interweave, focusing on a wholeness and balance that could not yet be understood. The longing for my true home and love were ever-present, all-pervading and ongoing.

Much like a mountain stream, instinct guided me onward with the rush of the clear, cool water, once pure white snow on the mountaintop, letting go, trusting, rushing forward into the unknown, changing and finally evaporating to return to the Divine Creator, ready once again to become pure, white snow.

When I was in tune with nature, releasing all conscious thoughts, I felt released from this dimension, at one with everyone and everything. Being in this space my true purpose emerged, guiding me to enjoy with others the harvest of my bountiful spiritual life, this book. I must take back my power of choosing by my free will, from the plethora of possibilities that God has gifted me with in this life, then I will live free.

It was time for me to establish a relationship with Sedona and its residents. A spiritual book store seemed to be the best way for me to connect with the like-minded, leading me to my still favorite place called Crystal Magic. The whole atmosphere was so inviting and so healing that hours went by perusing books and exploring the many semi-precious rocks and stones.

I looked for and found a statuesque Buddha sculpting in a sitting position. Finding the statue brought back the memories of the Buddhist temple I attended in Seattle. I enjoyed the teachings that started out so simply at their inception and ended up so third dimensional and complicated in their application to the linear world. Taking the simple approach, which is what I believe was the intent of Buddha, the cause of suffering is wanting. We are in a society of immediate gratification and living beyond our means. If we pay attention in mindfulness of our thoughts, our speech, our actions, our work and where we place our effort, we may come to enlightenment. It is that simple and yet that complicated.

Security, in this consciousness, demands ownership. This can create stagnation that will bind our thoughts and actions. Let home be a base but never a purpose or our limitations will control us. Maybe that is why I have been guided toward moving many times, to show me the truth in these words.

Wherever I go, my home is within me. This way I am always home whether sleeping in a tent or on a floor with a blanket. I know that my home is embodied in the whole Earth and, indeed, in the whole universe.

My understanding from the teachings is that human birth is a precious gift; our body that we are so enamored with will soon die and turn to dust; the results of the law of Karma, that whatever we do will return to us, so we must plant good seeds; the society that we have been programmed to live in creates suffering, for us to rise above and then assist others who choose to wake up.

The essence of my being is simplicity. The peace and love that come from choosing a life guided by Buddha's teachings are a living testimony. Each year brings a deeper understanding of myself, therefore, a deeper, more meaningful appreciation of others. When I lived in Seattle, the Buddhist Temple drew me to it, like I belonged. There was such gentleness and acceptance of who I am, no questions asked and no explanations necessary. I was welcomed with open, sincere love by the ever smiling Master Lu, who with an interpreter, granted me an audience. His message was very short and simple, You are very close to the Buddha which means the awakened or enlightened one, the one who knows. Awakened means with no attachments and using mindful actions, knowing that happiness occurs only in our thoughts. In this state of consciousness, there is no ego, only the final truth. Each of us is not only capable of such a form of being, but we are encouraged to allow such a state of awareness into our lives, should we so choose.

In a famous story, the Buddha was asked,
"Are you a god?"
"No", he replied.
"Are you a saint?"
"No."
"Then, what are you?"
"I am awake."

He meant that he was able to see who he was, where he was and what was going on around him because he was no longer blinded by belief systems.

At times, words of wisdom based on various teachings and experiences such as Buddhism have flowed from my mouth. They are understood in my mind but not always apparent in my actions. Knowing and then living a truth may be what we call bringing the kingdom of Heaven to Earth. Unfortunately, I still flounder, being guided by stubbornness and will rather than by knowingness.

Sedona had such a powerful energy, so forcefully exerted that I found living outside of the immediate area to be very desirable until I became accustomed. People flocked to the vortexes that were located at areas like Bell Rock, Airport Mesa and Boynton Canyon, to name a few. The people I talked to either felt a quantum shift in healing or sometimes a powerful nausea if they weren't ready for such high vibrations. In my case, there was no nausea but the word light-headed certainly applied.

I stayed in Sedona for another six months after being fired, spending a lot of time with my dear old friend Kushi who groomed herself on the deck chair, warming in the sun. This was her favorite place since, for once, she could feel the freedom of being outside without any intrusions from dogs or other animals. Little did the birds who flew over the deck warning her off know that she was not only declawed, but she didn't have a killer bone in her body. One bird came every day, seeming to develop a very sweet friendship and trust with her.

The old, familiar feeling of an upcoming move came over me again. It was as if I had skipped a step by not moving to North Carolina, a place that called to me while still living in Arkansas. Having ignored the pull to this area, it was important for me to now fulfill this guidance.

Sedona held a place for me of fine-tuning my energies, bringing forth new buds from my soul seed, uniting events with lessons, to see if I had set myself free from them. We each have what I call emotional buttons that, when pushed, give us the choice between reacting or responding to the situation. Reaction brings about a negative emotion which can lead to arguing, fighting, and finding the other person in the position of being wrong. Responding is being with the experience in communication, love and compassion, leading to growth and understanding rather than the separation of anger.

Sometimes I created my own symbolism. A finale to my time in Sedona came when attending a movie one day. As I approached the ticket window, I saw a large, golden, scarab shell sitting by the open ticket window. This was not only a very rare insect but hardly ever seen in this country, so I have been told. It felt like I had been given the symbol of a completion, like a reward for a job well done.

9

North Carolina

New, healthy buds spring forth

A brief period of time, but a very long journey, encompassed my next guided adventure as I headed for North Carolina. The apartment I had called ahead to reserve for our arrival turned out to be owned by a slum landlord. It was an old, stone cabin that used to be a motel who knows how long ago. Most rentals in the area didn't accept cats, but this one did and there was a roof over our heads.

The two-unit condos lined a half circle drive where I almost expected to see a new Model T pulling in for the night. We moved in and set about making this space a temporary home. To say that the units were ancient was putting it mildly. There were gaps and holes in the walls, especially in the kitchen which also housed much mold bringing forth my allergies.

There was no display of friendliness from the neighbors and I knew there would be no commonality after seeing their windows which had rakishly hanging sheets to shut out the sun. On occasion their two cats would peek out of the unscreened window and run hurriedly out into the grassy area, as they too displayed an unfriendly demeanor.

One day while sitting on the throne, I saw movement out of the corner of my eye and was startled to see a very large, black spider sitting on the sink a few inches from me. At first there was an uneasiness, then I noticed that he was just sitting there quietly. Knowing that this was his home and I was the intruder and not wanting to harm him, we started a don't bother policy which seemed to work for both of us. He would appear on the side of the old kitchen sink when I was doing dishes, sitting there almost as though he considered me to be his roommate. Maybe he was a little lonesome and looking for the company of someone to hang out with. He began to feel like a friend that I missed when he was not present.

In a quote from a painting my friend had in Illinois, it stated, "Who is rich? He who enjoys his portion." With the enjoyment of my portion, I explored Waynesville, a small town high in the Smokey Mountains. Charming shops filled with art work, earthy, animal-oriented gifts, and a bakery where the smell from fresh baked bread permeated the area, inviting me in to be greeted with "New in town?" Warm feelings were extended from the residents who were mostly middle-aged, retired couples who seemed to enjoy life. I loved it!

I often visited the Violet Flame bookstore, one of the area's spiritually motivated gathering places. One day I was introduced to a lady who felt very familiar, maybe from another life that must have been based in Karma. After telling her about my current living space, she offered me a room to rent in her home until I would soon find another place to live. Avoiding paying another month's rent was my motive but, as it turned out, it cost me more. My usual demeanor of being a loner using strict discernment, gave in to acceptance, leading me to make a very unlikely decision. Arriving at her home with Kushi and all of my belongings, she informed me that she had changed her mind. I was dumbfounded. Either we did, indeed, have Karma or she was rowing with one oar. I quickly called the slum landlord and asked if I could move back. My friend, the black spider, was nowhere to be found.

I reminded myself that the basis of life is freedom, the objective is joy and the result of life is growth. As I was taking my power back bit by bit, I knew enough not to worry about circumstances I couldn't control.

One week, urged by my guides to take Kushi for a walk downtown, I slipped her in the pet pouch that had one slot for her tail and two for her hind legs. She faced forward so she was able to greet the people who stopped to admire her. She loved it. One lady who stopped to pet her told me that she had three cats and found Himalayans to be very beautiful and special. Instinct guided me to ask her if she knew of a place for rent. Displaying perfect guidance in action, she was on her way to play bridge with a lady who had a guest house recently vacated. Following her in the car, I was overwhelmed with excitement when I saw this enchanting guest cottage located in her side yard. Big, three-story high pine trees were suspended over and around the cottage, as if they were guarding and protecting this very unique and cozy place. The rooms were furnished, and best of all, the rent was $50 less than the former undesirable place. Intuition, trust and faith always work even though I get side-tracked once in awhile. When I expected nothing, what I received was always perfect.

The five months I lived in the small community of Lake Junaluska were filled with detoxifying and healing of my physical body, releasing remnants of anger and finding and revealing the softer, more feminine side of myself. It felt like Kushi and I were in a cocoon while being loved, preparing for a new adventure as a butterfly. The caterpillar lives its life crawling on the Earth until time to build a cocoon around its physical self, hibernating and changing into a beautiful butterfly, able to fly and be free from this dimension while still living in it. The Divine Process was guiding me in this sweet hideaway, full circle to a more intimate remembrance of who I am.

My landlady was 82 years old and had the spirit and energy of a woman 20 years her junior. Fulfilling her duties as the widow of a Methodist minister, she would carry out her role of peace maker, healer and angelic being, giving of energies to help others. Sometimes when she arrived home, I would share my homemade chicken soup and chocolate dessert, much to her delight. While I was busy writing my book, she was performing her job as an angel. For a brief time we shared our gifts with each as we served humanity.

A strange feeling about not having a job crept back into my thoughts. I reminded myself that this was a time for healing which took a lot of energy and effort. Then I found one of the quotes I had collected over the years:

> *Success has nothing to do with hard work! This is the law of least effort. There is no effort involved. Do less and accomplish more. Do nothing and accomplish everything.* — AUTHOR UNKNOWN

Okay, I can live with this philosophy. My book was starting to take form with very little effort. I was prioritizing my life and thoughts and forgot about the job.

After living through the process of releasing the poisons that had been stored in my body cells with a special diet and herbs and a growing familiarity with the bathroom, the beauty of nature called me outside to explore. I drove north toward Black Mountain and arrived at a domed building on its high mountain perch, quite secluded and very quiet. The light center had been recommended to me, so I opened the door and was greeted by a soft-spoken man who had met a friend of mine, Douet, an artist who displayed some of his most imaginative, spiritually-guided painting on the walls.

After a tour of the building, he took me to a room where various colored spotlights attuned to each separate chakra adorned the walls. Sitting down on a modern white leather seat, the light show and the odyssey of becoming at one with the music and lights began. I left feeling refreshed, relaxed and again very blessed with the abundance of the healing universe. It was free.

To see more is to become more.
—TEILHARD DeCHARDIN

The name of a town called Franklin kept coming up in conversations, so my next trip was to head southwest and take in the beauty of the waterfalls abundant in that area. After driving up what seemed like a never-ending curvy road, Bridal Falls loomed in front of me just around a corner. I was a little disappointed to find that the falls were no more than water dripping down off an overhang.

With high hopes, I drove one mile further to Dry Falls that more than made up for my expectations, although the name was misleading. I walked down the tree-lined path, fall leaves of gold, red and orange rustling under my feet. I felt the latent mist of the falls and heard the roar of the water as I approached. The water was so loud that it was impossible to talk to other visitors, so we smiled, nodded and moved on.

On the way back down the mountain, there was a place to pan for precious stones that abound in the area. Being a rock and stone lover, I joyfully spent two hours screening out garnets, amethysts, crystals and, most importantly, had time to settle my motion sick stomach.

My life's path may seem a little erratic to most people. Learning that I am very loved and that my highest and best good is behind my guidance gives me implicit faith and great joy.

One day on my weekly downtown Waynesville walks, I felt pulled into a distinguished, high-priced clothing store. Knowing that I didn't have the means to buy, the sale table drew me right to it. A big find: a bag with my daughter-in-law's favorite colors and at a price that I could afford.

As I approached the lady behind the counter, my reason for driving 2,000 miles to live in North Carolina for six months was revealed to me. There was a feeling of familiarity, something about her that was magnetic and magical. We talked, almost immediately recognizing each other from other lifetimes. After that, I returned to the store three times and had tea at her home, as we discussed matters of spirit and who we are. Not knowing why spirit pointed out the way for her to work in this store, but very faithful to her guidance, she contributed her artistic touch to the store, working overtime, going above and beyond for the good of the store. Unfortunately, her boss never acknowledged her extra efforts. When we met, she too knew the reason why the universe had set up our meeting place.

Our lives were all so intrinsically intertwined that the one small change in my life, that of moving to Arizona instead of North Carolina at the time she started work in the store, affected her plans, much like a pebble that is dropped into a stream affects the water by radiating circles out from the point of impact.

Purpose fulfilled, my pull to move back to Arizona came almost immediately. I lived my life as it came to me with faith and trust that all is in good order. I had found an old friend but was not meant to live near her for some reason. We talked on the phone and sent e-mails often, to keep in touch.

The small, still voice inside spoke clearly and loudly as more layers of self, like onion layers, dissolved and disappeared. What a strange feeling, as stated in The Shadow Of Me, peeling away layers that once were perceived as self only to find a stranger underneath.

Camp Verde

*Bringing forth the sweet nectar from
the fruits that bear seeds for the
beginning of another cycle*

Kushi and I arrived in Camp Verde, Arizona and followed
detailed directions that finally took us to a dirt road that
dead-ended where a small house nestled in the side of a hill
overlooking the Verde River and the Mingus Mountains. We
were to live here for two and a half years while I finished
this book.

Before I left North Carolina, trusting the truth within,
I called David and his wife to ask them to find a place for me
to rent in and around the Cottonwood-Sedona area. This
wasn't the easiest of challenges since the rent in these areas is
outrageously high. They took my request very seriously and,
on their precious few days of rest, looked for just the right
place, thoughtfully sending me pictures of the house and
setting. My contribution to the search was to ask my

higher self and spirits to guide them. They did and the space was perfect.

One day, a week before my planned departure, I was watching television amidst the confusion of packed boxes, when a voice came to me saying, pack the truck and leave Sunday, which was the day after tomorrow. Thanks to El Niño, the weather had been very erratic, to say the least. As it turned out, Sunday was the last window of good traveling weather for the whole month.

When I announced that I was moving, the most loving landlady that I had experienced in my travels took me out to dinner at a local, cherished restaurant that specialized in fried chicken. We had an all-you-can-eat good time. As we exchanged hugs, I felt very sad about leaving this warm friendship with such a charming, intelligent woman. We gave each other another hug as she recited a prayer of peace and well-being.

I am very thankful for my 1983 pick-up that has so carefully and safely carried Kushi and me with our few belongings on this and the last three moves from state to state.

A journey of a thousand miles begins with a single step. — CONFUCIUS

It was a miracle inspired by love to move into our new space that had been so carefully selected for us. There was a living room and kitchen with window-lined walls, two small rooms and a bathroom. The deck view proudly displayed the trees, outlining the oh-so precious water in the river and the ranches with thorough-bred horses, pecan farms and broad expanses of fields with cows, horses, goats and pigs.

I had come full circle back to a place where I had lived before: from the planting of the seed to the time of harvest, from the alpha to the omega, from the caterpillar to the cocoon, to the snake and the shedding of another skin. Returning to the same setting in familiar territory gave me insight into growth and progress toward remembering who I am. The truth is that once I realized that there were no definitive answers and trusted the process, day by day, it set me free to flow in the moment. Expressing from knowing, I felt a great sense of relief that expressed itself in an almost hysterical laughter. Life was so easy when I got out of the way.

> *Noble virtue is not the abstinence of life but the embracing of it. For one who abstains from life has an empty soul. One who is immersed in life dreams the illusions and the adventures and grasps the wisdom.* — AUTHOR UNKNOWN

Possibly one of the blessings of being in a physical body is to find the limits and go beyond to another side of knowing. We are being asked to access a state of being that is beyond our five senses in order to allow Spirit to express through this body, bringing what we call Heaven on Earth. What a magnificent gift we have brought with us to reveal within ourselves and then share with the world! Keep in mind that no one is ever alone in this journey of bringing our gifts of love to this dimension.

Living in Arizona, a dry desert area, water is a very revered commodity. One day as I was moving the hose to water the blackberry bushes, I noticed two snails intertwined with one another on the hose connection where water was leaking out. I observed them leaving their shells almost completely and was amazed at their large size. One that I assumed was the male was about four inches long with antennae about one inch long. The other a translucent, almost pinkish color, I believed to be a female. They became aware of my presence and retracted back into their shells. After convincing them that I meant no harm, they revealed their trust and understanding by again coming out of their shells almost completely, writhing in the moist grass.

Whenever I ran water for them, they responded without fear and allowed me to take notice of their trust that we are all one. When I feel loved and safe, I too come out of my shell to reveal the inner beauty of my soul. We learn about ourselves most powerfully by watching the instinctive flow and trust of nature. As the snails, my body temple is also my temporary home.

> *We must move on to recognize both the integrity of the individual and the underlying unity that connects our species to all other living things.*
> — R. BUCKMINSTER FULLER

> *In the beginning of all things, wisdom and knowledge were with the animals: for Tirawa, the one above did not speak directly to man. He sent certain animals to tell men that he showed himself through the beasts, and that from them, and from the stars and the sun and the moon, man should learn. Tirawa spoke to man through his works.*
> — EAGLE CHIEF LETAKOTS-LESA

As I began my morning walk down the long, dirt road from my house, I observed the blue herons, dogs, cats and other foraging animals who found fresh mounds of soil each morning announcing the entrance to the gopher holes, much to the satisfaction of their hunger. The neighbor's dogs Luna, a miniature Doberman Pinscher, and Toast, a mixed Golden Retriever, happy to see someone out this early in the morning, came running with wagging tails to greet me. They ran erratically in and around me for awhile until they tired of the game and headed home. Blue herons with their lofty, at least six-foot viewing height, pranced around in the garden looking for food which sometimes came in the form of field mice and other rodents.

As I walked down the street to one of the fence-lined fields, I was greeted by Hambone, the pot belly pig who seemed to be in a continual state of ingesting food; the two white geese who, when approached, become very agitated and took on their watch dog mode; and the horses, Felice being the most friendly, ambling in my direction, turning and running upon my approach, in anticipation of a gourmet treat of either carrots or whole wheat bread. In the purity of their being, they shared a sweet friendship with me that I will never forget.

On my walks during the monsoon season, my nostrils filled with the all-pervading odor of moistness from wet grass and saturated soil. It created a heaviness in my breathing and, even though it was only six in the morning, sweat poured from my body. Fluffy, moist-laden clouds hung in and around the valleys formed by the Mingus Mountains, like feather boas casually thrown around their girth. As I walked on the path between giant, cottonwood trees and lush vegetation by the river, breathing in the aroma of green, I felt at one, grounded into the Earth and one with nature. These are the unsung heroes who quietly do their bidding holding the soil, cleansing the air and providing shade, while nourishing and being one with the soul of us all. A connecting of Heaven and Earth in a balance only nature knows at this time. Back home, dripping with sweat from the high humidity, I typed the words and whole thoughts that flooded into my mind before the day's activities began.

Rainbow Warriors

The stillness that comes just before a storm
A quietening announcing nature's intention
to nourish the Earth.
The soft whisper of the trees as the wind winds its way
through the leaves.
The giving forth of the outpouring of nourishment from God
... the rain falls.
The music of the whispering leaves, the drops of rain
reverberating as they meet the Earth,
create a symphony for the heart and soul.
Green turns to golden-green as the dust of the old
is washed away revealing the wisdom and
awareness of the new.
The water bearer has again nourished all of nature bringing
forth the beauty that feeds our souls
and food that nourishes our bodies.
Can we not see what is before our eyes?
Can we not feel in our hearts and souls
the love pouring forth?
Awaken, Rainbow Warriors, dear ones, and carry the waters
forth from our souls.
For is it not the reflection of the sun of God upon
the water mist that creates the rainbows?

I am so thankful for these mornings and for being granted a period of time on Earth with a day-to-day mindfulness of our participation with and connection to everyone, everything and all.

Under the false assumption that I had arrived at a place of healing where I went beyond reacting to having my buttons pushed, shock hit me as remnants of dysfunctional aspects of self flooded into my awareness for forgiveness and release. Sitting quietly for a period of time asking for clarity, I was reminded of the following analogy: We are like onions with many layers to be peeled away. Each layer is ready to be taken away as we are emotionally ready to release it. Feeling the love and safety of my present space, I was ready to release the energies of lessons that had already been learned. It felt like climbing a mountain and then reaching a plateau. This time it was easier as the memories of events that made up my individual life came forward into my conscious mind. I was told to not look beyond myself for the truth, for it can only be within the seed of my soul, left to be discovered.

As I experience letting go of dysfunctional behavior, my understanding of the process is to acknowledge the behavior, thank it for the lessons, remembering not to repeat it again and to release it in love without judgment.

My grandson joined the family on August 15, 1998 at 4:49 in the morning. While waiting for his entrance into this world, my granddaughter, Miranda and I brought coffee, sodas, ice and water to the birthing room where my daughter-in-law was in hard labor and my son David was in suspended animation from lack of sleep and excitement. It was such a privilege to be included and welcomed into the pre delivery room where the baby's heartbeat was being monitored along with the measured intensity of the labor pains.

It became obvious that my grandson would be coming onto the scene very soon. What seemed like such a short time later, the doors of the delivery room opened and out walked David holding his new son, tears rolling down his cheeks. He had just witnessed the birth of a new soul coming into this life. My daughter-in-law, courageously awake throughout the delivery, came out smiling, relieved that he was a healthy little boy. My granddaughter, Miranda was so proud of her new brother that the mothering instinct kicked in with the request to hold him.

My son and daughter came into my life to remind me of
who I am. My grandchildren arrived at a time when I am
again looking at life as though through the eyes of a child.
Life was good that day. The sense of peace filled me to
overflowing at that moment. Only now, my participation in
this life is from one whose eyes and heart have left the
innocence of childhood.

My life returned to a daily routine which included my
morning walks. The scenery, as the seasons go from summer
to fall to winter, brought an ever-changing panorama of
Mother Nature's beauty: the melodious song of the meadow
lark, the staccato woo woo of the turtle doves along with the
ongoing chatter of a group of unidentified birds forms an
unplanned chorus, as I stepped out of my front door for a
brisk walk.

Staying present in the moment opens up a whole, new
world that has always been there, but not realized, as layers of
self heal and fall away, the blossoming seed opens to the
discovery of my spiritual rhythm.

The furrows of rich, black soil envelop the seeds of winter
wheat that, in a few days, will burst forth full of promise. The
small, green and fragile plants form a lush green carpet over
the field that has held and grown other plantings in the
nourishing mastery of Mother Earth. Even the seeds that fall
by the road and struggle in an unfriendly medium, gain
strength in their early development that serves them well as
they grow to maturity. The produce shack at Windmill Farms
stands naked and deserted after the bountiful, summer glut of
vegetables, during the winter, its purpose unfulfilled.

Likened unto the winters of my life when seemingly all
purpose and direction had vanished and times when I called
upon the faith and courage so bravely won up to this place in

my life, I held the awareness that there will always be remnants of healing coming up to restore myself to original integrity.

The cattle grazed quietly, seemingly content with their station in life. The irrigation ditches were emptied of their water, revealing rocks, gravel, tumbleweeds and various discarded refuse once hidden in their watery grave.

As I approached a pasture where a horse and her young colt had been confined in a space barely large enough to turn around, my chest tightened and tears welled up in my eyes. The feelings were familiar and yet not so welcome, as memories of the past filled my thoughts and bubbled to the surface to no longer be denied. Always the proper lady longing to be loved for who I am, the real me inside felt trapped, looking for a way out. With my pressing lack of being unable to touch the most tender of places in my heart that yearn for intimacy with life and others, I was filled with sadness. No one seemed to notice or even care that I was being pulled and directed in ways according to the high level of self-interest of others. I felt lost and there was no one who could find me but me. It was my lesson and the only way for me was out.

As I remember from my childhood, any time that feelings of sadness and grief or fear came up, I was sent to my bedroom to cry alone. There was such a denial of feelings and any loss of control in my life up to this point taught me that these displays were not acceptable. Seeking familiar expression, the same atmosphere was also true in my marriage where my feelings were not acknowledged.

My emotions were buried, becoming the basis for behavior that closed off my heart and loving expressions. Having a well of uncried tears needing to be released,

I carried on with my life unable to express myself fully, hiding my true feelings.

One afternoon tears started flowing out of my eyes and I felt totally out of control. A deep, almost primal scream of grief came up from the bowels of my being, gushing forth as a guttural scream that went on and on. I was conscious of what was happening, but became a detached observer. After a long period of unknown time, my body went limp from the amount of energy that had been expelled. A great healing had taken place and a freedom never before felt in this lifetime filled me with joy.

> *The process of self-forgiveness is complete when we let go of what we have done and celebrate what we have become. The process of forgiving others is complete when we let go of what they have done and celebrate the wisdom we have gained through the difficult experience they have facilitated for us.*
> — JOAN BORYSENKO, PH.D., GUILT IS THE TEACHER, LOVE IS THE LESSON. WARNER BOOKS, INC.

I have been reading from, *Pocketful of Miracles and Guilt Is The teacher, Love Is The Lesson,* for a year ever since my sister Connie gave them to me for my birthday. Finding so many synchronicities with the book that I had been writing for years encouraged me that the message of healing is coming through many of us to share as a possibility for others, in their free will, to learn from.

You may be wondering what happened to the horse and her colt. Over a one year period I was in contact with the animal shelter, the police department and the Arizona Livestock Association numerous times for intervention. My neighbors who owned the horses stopped speaking to me, as I addressed the abuse of these two powerful, gentle animals.

People seem to think that breaking the spirit of an animal is more desirable than loving cooperation. Some day may the consciousness of the Earth be that of love.

My first step toward freedom came after leaving my 27 year marriage 20 years ago. I didn't begin to live and love until later in my life. We only know what we live until the courage comes up to change the situation. I took a deep breath and the sadness disappeared. My kinship and purpose with the horses realized, I moved on. Drawing closer to the platform deck by my front door, my eyes met with the splendor and grandeur of the Mingus Mountains against the deep blue background of the sky. It was a fitting visual end to my commune with nature and the healing that had been bestowed upon me that morning. It felt like I was seeing them for the first time.

Like hiking up a mountain, the process of releasing judgment of self and others was gradual. For me, reaching the pinnacle represented an immediate shift that took place as I again felt a never before known freedom. I am an infinite creator, always seeking balance from the choices I make and, hopefully, learning from the resulting experiences. That there is no good or bad, right or wrong, I understood philosophically, but not in my heart and whole being. When I am being true to myself, I am being true to everyone. When I am at peace with myself, I am at peace with everyone. What I perceive as anger from others is really anger coming from myself, yet mirrored in others. I can observe others with detachment or allow them to push my buttons, revealing the anger within myself.

A Navajo Indian told a story about how his people deal with an angry child. An elder, usually a grandparent, approaches the child asking why he is so angry with himself, putting the focus where it belongs.

On one of my walks, I saw coming toward me a tall, stately being in the form of a 91 year old woman. We approached each other and immediately began talking as if we were old friends, both acknowledging precognition of our meeting. The conversation flowed easily, bringing forth a commonality in our ways of being and our beliefs. I felt blessed to be in her presence, walking her back to the house where there was a gathering for a funeral of a family member, in order to prolong our conversation. When I was asked how I spent my time, this book title was shared with her. She very calmly looked into my eyes and said that it will be published and help a lot of people find their way. It was said with such bold certainty that any vestige of doubt on my part easily disappeared.

Everything is speaking to us all of the time, be it animals, nature, people or situations. They are verbally or quietly teaching us who we are and our place in the scheme of things. Pay attention! Life is magical! Don't take anything for granted.

Living in this lush valley by the Verde River, I felt encapsulated in a protective womb of love, guidance and healing. I hesitated but intuitively started saying good-bye, ready to be released from this place that has contained, enveloped and generated my seed of the Divine. Good-bye Felice, my gentle, loving friend the horse. Good-bye to the mother and her colt who have served as a symbol, reflecting my own pain and healing. Good-bye to Hambone, forever sweet, running at the sound of my voice to accept my offering of bread and carrots. Good-bye to the meadowlarks who serenaded me every morning as I walked, in the beauty of the landscape of growing crops and large green expanses of wilderness and mountains. The light made known through Divine Inspiration as I awakened, revealed true purpose. Somewhere along the way, I found myself.

In order to actualize our life purpose we must maintain a continual awareness that life is a gift of inestimable value and that we are caretakers of that gift. — CHEROKEE TEACHER AND HEALER DHYANI YWAHOO

It seemed like only overnight since the irrigation ditches that were flowing freely, gave the possibility of life to the newly planted seeds, as the ditches were drained of their life-giving force. The seeds awaited the water needed to carry their intended gifts into fruition and the giving of their fruits. Another cycle had begun. I walked that morning, encompassed in the feeling of wholeness as tears of joy rolled down my cheeks. I was growing home as my Divine Seed came forth in all its glory, blossoming into true self-expression.

Kushi

One journey is over but another is beginning

When Kushi died, at 14 years of age, her death became a catalyst for releasing any other tears stored from hiding my true feelings. I must be patient and compassionate with myself and allow.

Her Sanskrit name fulfilled its meaning through the presence of the dear friend in my life, Kushi, which means joy and happiness. Not being aware of my upcoming participation in circumstances that were beyond my control may have been in the form of a gift.

Kushi, who came into my life as friend, teacher and healer, was preparing to leave her physical shell. She had stood by me through thick and thin and I could do no less for her. I decided that unless she was uncomfortable with pain, I had no right to interfere with her process of going from the physical body through the veil to a higher and lighter place, for this was a very personal journey.

Thoughts of accepting what is, being detached with unconditional love and respecting everyone's journey, flowed from my mouth. I had, to the best of my ability, lived by these words. Now, when faced with the passing of my dear friend, these words came back to haunt me. Grieving is natural but thinking that I had any control over how and when she will leave is ego. I was there as her friend to comfort and support her. Even in her physical death, she was my teacher.

The flesh melted away from her fragile, thinning body. Tuna, her favorite treat, was left on the plate because she could no longer eat without the reprisal of pain from her bowels that had not functioned for the last few days. Was it necessary to leave this world only after the gradually painful experience of a failing body? The word release kept filling my mind. Was I holding on to her? Was she waiting for my acceptance of her death before she would go?

Kushi was so enlightened that the spirit shining from her eyes and expressing through her actions, fooled the first vet into believing that she was still okay. He ignored the loss of almost four pounds from her small nine pound body and recommended a shot to make her feel better. At this point, I accepted the shot in the hope that it would help her. I left his office feeling happy that she was still alive and sadness about the truth ... that her spirit was strong and willing, but her body was full of pain.

A few days later I went to another vet who took x-rays, revealing three tumors along her spine, one of which was pressing on the nerve that allowed bowel movements. At 14 years of age, in a lot of pain and with only suffering ahead, I chose the most loving way for her to leave. I had to be honest with myself, loving and fair to Kushi. Euthanasia was the only answer and yet an undesirable answer. Getting up in

the middle of the night to soothe her as she let out cries of
pain,
I could only be happy about her dropping the body temple
which was giving her a joyless existence. The vet said that her
heart was very strong and the dying process, if not
interrupted, would be prolonged and painful.

We were approaching a long Labor Day weekend and
I selfishly decided that spending these last few days with her
were very important to me. Saturday she stood in front of
me, the black pupils expanding to cover the beautiful blue
color of her eyes. She stared at me, like many times before
when there was to be communication between us, saying
telepathically that she was ready to leave. Her normal
behavior of cuddling with me every night had been
interrupted by the pain and discomfort she had been feeling
the last few nights. September 4, the night before she made
me aware of her willingness to leave, the normal routine
returned, letting me cuddle with her and rub her stomach.
Later, I became aware that this was her way of saying
good-bye.

That Saturday I felt very tired, having slept very little for
the last week, but all of a sudden, strength flowed through
my body as though I was being guided by puppet strings.
I called the vet, the crematorium and took a shower. I had
already bathed Kushi to make her feel better after some of
the invasive tests she had endured at the vets. Her wet fur
revealed how very thin and frail her body had become.
I cried.

When we arrived at the vet's office, I held her up outside
to see the vibrant fall colors of the trees and distant
mountains, wanting her last memory on the Earth to be one
of great beauty. After wrapping her in the sweater decorated

with cats that my sister had given me, Dr. Redman gave her
the shot to relax her body so that the final injection would not
be so traumatic. I rubbed her head and face, telling her again
about the journey that she would take through the veil into
the light and then home with family and loved ones. Now she
was free from pain.

I took her to the pet crematorium 20 miles to another
town, sobbing and feeling very lost without her presence by
my side, alive. Coming home from the crematorium, walking
in the door, tears poured down my cheeks. The house felt so
empty. Then I heard a loud meow as if to say, don't worry,
I am okay. Relieved that she would still be here but in another
form unseen by my eyes, I placed her ashes in a blue urn
placed on my alter with the statue of Buddha. A year later her
ashes were spread under a climbing rose bush outside my
back door.

I didn't realize just how much I depended on Kushi's
company, companionship and love. In hind sight, it was
obvious that her health had been failing for awhile and I had
been in denial. After a month of grieving her loss, I came to
the conclusion that it was more important and loving to
honor the fourteen years of life that she was willing to share
with me, rather than mourning the day of her death. My
heart poured forth words which were said over her ashes, to
honor her life.

Kushi arrived on Earth on August 8, 1984
Kushi journeyed home on September 5, 1998

You can never really pass out of my life, because of all the
memories I have in which you have played a part.
You have filled my heart and life
with blessings by your presence and taught me what it
felt like to be loved unconditionally, with courage,
faithfulness and bravery, leaving me a better person than
before you came into my life.
I miss your greetings at the door and our times of talking
and cuddling. Having your beautiful energy and sweet self
with me has made our places of residence a home.
I hold you in my heart with love, releasing only the body
temple which now resides in an urn holding only ashes.
So, good-bye for now, sweet face. A good-bye is followed
by our power to meet again which is a given for those of us
who love each other. You lived a good and long life and
are complete with the Earth. So, good-bye, dear Kushi.

Periods of grieving still come up but the healing took
place more profoundly when I knew that Kushi was still
present in my life, only in a form not yet apparent to my eyes.

O

Circle of Possibilities

My understanding is that here on the Earth we live by the law of free will. To have free will there must be choices available. Pondering this thought one day, a vision came to me of a circle with truth written in the center.

The Divine Presence, umbrella phrase for all belief systems, wanted to experience self, so the Earth school was seeded with our souls. The law of nature is a circle, continuous, giving and receiving. When the mind is kept open to a complete circle of possibilities, one may reach a level of wisdom that will create movement from one circle to the next, ascending the spiral to the Divine Mind ... Growing Home. The moment we start creating special points, ideas and distinctions, we exile ourselves from the state of God consciousness and miss the infinite freedom of free will.

On the day we are born, our journey home begins. The question is, where is home? I had an ongoing dream in my childhood. School is out; I walk toward home; turn down the street where I live; there is no home to be found. Panic runs

through my entire body, waking me up to a pounding heart
and body sweats. Maybe my higher self was showing me,
even then, where my true home resides. My belief is that
when we are given a physical body, (what I call a body
temple) not all of our soul energy comes to reside in it. Some
energy remains in the higher realms (higher self) to
occasionally be accessed for guidance. In all the times that
I have moved, my journey was about learning trust and faith,
not seeking a home in a place. Now I know that it was my
true path to me, my true home which was always right here,
my soul, Divine Seed.

I had no idea where my inner and outer travels would take
me. Armed with blind faith and grand bravado, after I left my
27 year marriage, knowing that the guiding hand offered to
me would show the way. Being veiled, I was unaware
consciously of the process, for how could there be an
authentic understanding with knowledge of the end purpose?

Taking one step at a time, ignoring the goal, focusing
always on the process and moment at hand, I knew that it was
necessary to allow and not get in the way. Being a visual
person, let me share an example that came to me as I relaxed
into the healing at hand.

A hot air balloon glides silently over the Earth's terrain.
I sigh with relief as another sand bag filled with old patterns
of fear and guilt are released from its girth. As each bag is
dropped, the balloon rises up softly, gaining freedom from
the earthly pull of gravity, the energies that have kept me
asleep and involved in the third dimension. I also know that
to enjoy with others this state of mind so hard won, it is
necessary to stay here on this grand and beautiful Earth.

"We are not here to fit into the dream," my friend William
David who started The Esoteric Center in Houston would

say, but to "awaken ourselves and assist others who are firmly ensconced in this consciousness." We are here to remind each other of who we are. Who better to heal us than those we know and love so deeply, our true, spiritual family. By serving each other, we become free.

Profound gifts came cloaked as lessons that my soul had chosen for me: guiding me to meet old karmic relationships, listening to my guidance, following it without fear or question, living authentically by speaking my own truth, not interfering in others' choices, and finding out who I am by moving away from my old life and the games that kept the dynamics of fear and control alive in my family and again in my marriage. What I had always thought intellectually, I now feel in my heart. Although we are each unique unto ourselves, we are all one.

I moved from state to state, breaking up old ways of thinking and old ways of being to live life with more purpose, free from the societal pull of sameness, and free finally, to find my own voice.

Now I live life as it comes to me, knowing that I am only a participant, an actor playing an agreed-upon part. I am living in the moment, asking for what I want and joyfully accepting that which comes to me. When we struggle with that which we have been given, we create our own suffering.

I am unplugging and deprogramming from the third dimensional information and so-called facts we were given that were then supported by parents, school, television, radio and advertising. Having no other recourse than to buy into the lies so blatantly given, we absorbed it all being so eager to learn about life on Earth.

*Coming out of the illusion, revealing those who would take
away our freedoms through their deeds, we bring an end to
their covert actions. The light made known through our
Divine Inspiration as we awaken, reveals their dark secrets
and sets us free from the demands of their tyranny.*

Embracing the circle of possibilities and destiny, I finally
felt safe enough to start living my soul's expression to the
extent that I knew who I was. Purpose fulfilled, whether it be
karmic, a reminder of true self and purpose, or the pleasure
of reuniting with old friends. People come and go in my life
and some stay as life rewarding friends forever. I am so
blessed!

We each have a Divine Seed of our own, growing home,
expanding in wisdom, developing to maturity; a process of
natural growth proceeding toward a source of radiated
energy: ... a place of origin. —Growing Home

Living from the awareness of owning our own power;
armed with faith and trust, we invite into our lives great
adventure.

All I can promise you is that it will be an amazing journey.

*The full impact of my request to
higher self, the Divine Presence
and Guides, didn't come into
fruition consciously until
I lived my journey and one turn of
the spiral on the wheel of
incarnation, in the Conclusion.*

Conclusion

The new seeds are dispersed, ready to begin their journey ... Growing Home

*Nature is setting seed, storing the energy of the
Light for future generations.
Likewise, our souls are coming to spiritual maturity ...
a flexible, gracious attitude that finds intense
joy in the very impermanence of life.*
—JOAN BORYSENKO, PH.D.,
POCKETFUL OF MIRACLES WARNER BOOKS, INC.

The pathway of life may be compared to the adventures
of climbing a mountain. During the times of major shifts in
my life, I was climbing up the vertical walls ascending toward
the soul self, remembering with each step who I am and my
purpose here on Earth. Then a plateau, a relatively level
surface, appeared ahead to offer a stable period of rest to
temporarily bring my journey to an end before taking the
initial steps on yet another vertical climb.

My own personal victories showed up again and again in
the form of shifts of consciousness which then guided me to
the completion of yet another cycle. I have left the illusion of
separateness and moved into an indivisible whole. The
sweetness of the wine of the fruits born of my seed encourage
the journey forward into the yet unknown reaches of
possibility. Throughout this life I have climbed the vertical
reaching plateaus many times, coming to the ultimate
purpose of completing the circle back to the beginning,

ready to begin yet another cycle. It is time to recognize as genuine and valid the spiritual credit gained from my courage and persistence.

On top of the mountain, out of the dense Earth's atmosphere, I am able to stand outside of myself, free from need, lust, and greed, free to be the detached observer. Now it is time for the birthing of my Divine Self for the giving of my soul's gifts. The seed bursts forth, blossoming into my utmost power.

> *You come to know God, not through what you know spiritually, but through your lack of attachment. Attachments are the key reason for our struggle. We are holding on tightly to something we think has value when, in truth, it doesn't and we won't let go when things change. So it is not essential that we have a lot of pain on the spiritual path and yet, with pain we do grow. We grow equally with happiness.* — ELIOTT JAMES, ATTAINING THE MASTERSHIP: ADVANCED STUDIES ON THE SPIRITUAL PATH

When the seed of our own develops and bears fruit, we share our gifts with the indivisible whole, of which we are a part. We are each truly a magnificent aspect of the Divine Presence.

The Greek word agape means being with and for another, but without attachment, without wanting and or fearing. It is that spacious place where all is accepted. There is nothing to hide. This is the fullest expression of daily human life.

I live my life as it comes to me, knowing that true spirituality is peaceful, nonintrusive, gentle, compassionate and humble. Having no attachments and knowing that the strength of shared vision will make our world over in light, I find that every destination is but a doorway to the next journey. A quote from, Tara Singh, in his book, *Gratefulness* offered me wise and gentle guidance toward my destination.

It is time to encourage the process of identification with the spirit in each other. We will learn to invoke this sacred presence that is our reality. To unfold the inherent capacity within each of us. This capacity is already present in each of us and is not born of further knowledge or learning. — TARA SINGH, GRATEFULNESS

I take full responsibility for my actions. I always keep appointments, showing up on time. I listen to what others have to say, incorporating that which is wise and loving into my life. I speak with honesty the possibilities that are my truth with discernment and open heart. I ask for what I want and accept gratefully that which I receive.

In spiritual life there is no momentum, we are always at the beginning. I agreed to come to the Earth as a willing participant. Every experience was carefully and with soul free-will chosen to bring me to who I am today, a part of the all that is.

We have come from the alpha to the omega, ready to signal Om, a sign to the Divine Presence that we are coming home in bringing Heaven to Earth. The return of the Divine Consciousness.

The written script of our play drama is complete. It is time for us to step out of duality into love and atonement, our true state of Being. No more sucking thumbs and dragging blankets. We stand naked before the all that is ... full of possibilities.

I have shared with you the wise words of others who have
so profoundly affected and enhanced my journey. It is
imperative that we each choose our own path, do our own
processing and learn our own lessons, lest it be an
empty victory.

Humanity is exalted as we reach enlightenment. It affects
all those who came before and those who come after.

Now the true meaning has revealed itself. The peaceful
valley, the rainbows, eagles, the waterfall, the gentle, sweet
smelling breeze, and the animals that I use as a form of
visualization and meditation were all aspects of self I was
seeking to remember and embrace. Life is a journey. It starts
the day you are born. The will and ego have guided and
protected me for over 69 years. Now it is time for them to
work freely with the soul's innate wisdom to give the gifts that
it came to Earth to give.

Fall, my favorite time of year, is upon us. There is a calm,
a silence, as nature releases the old and hibernates, only to
burst forth in the spring with renewed energy. Animals and
human beings rest from the quickening of the soul, to go
inside to reflect upon their choices, the experiences that
resulted from their choices. All is quiet as the renewal process
takes place. The days are shorter, the nights longer, the
weather colder, the birds migrate. There is a rhythm to all of
life that births the new and releases the old.

The seed bursts forth into a flowering fruit after its
completion again ready to set seed and begin a new journey.
After the long ascent up the mountain, arrival at the top
begins with a new, different seed setting for the next turn of
the spiral. The physical seed completes its cycle. The new
seed is a growing concept of Spirit spiraling on and on. Each
layer of the spiral announces a new beginning, coming from

physical moving on to a concept of mind, body and spirit. There is a beginning to completion, a never-ending story.

When this spiritual tour of life began 20 years ago, I asked the Divine guiding hand and my higher self to bring in all sources of imbalance and needed healing from this and other lifetimes to be released. They lovingly gifted me by fulfilling my request. I am very thankful.

As my journey began, I was standing amongst the trees. Moving out from under the trees, I looked, and saw that it was a forest all along.

Shutting down my computer, this book completed, the words on the screen tell me that it is going into hibernation. It reminds me of the feelings I now have as my path leads me into the waiting room.

A door opens. I feel drawn into the white mist over the threshold. There are no noticeable walls. I see no one. I hear no noise. I feel space filled with a perfect silence, protected and loved. And although I see no chair, I sit down with a sense that I have entered the waiting room.

There is a stranger in the house. It is me.

The Lord's Prayer

Aramaic Translation
A translation directly from the Aramaic into English
(rather than from Aramaic to Greek to Latin to English)

O Cosmic Birther of all radiance and vibration!
Soften the ground of our being and carve out a space
Within us where Your presence can abide.
Fill us with your creativity so that we may be
Empowered to bear the fruit of Your mission.
Let each of our actions bear fruit in accordance
with our desire.
Endow us with the wisdom to produce and share
What each being needs to grow and flourish.
Untie the tangled threads of destiny that bind us as we
Release others from the entanglement of past mistakes.
Do not let us be seduced by that which would divert us
From our true, purpose but illuminate the opportunities
of the present moment.
For You are the ground and the fruitful vision,
the birth-power and fulfillment,
As all is gathered and made whole once again.